Individual
Rights and Civic
Responsibility

THE RIGHT TO
BEAR ARMS

Michael A. Sommers

The Rosen Publishing Group, Inc.
New York

Published in 2001 by The Rosen Publishing Group, Inc.
29 East 21st Street, New York, NY 10010

First Edition

Cover photo © Archive Photography

Library of Congress Cataloging-in-Publication Data

Sommers, Michael A., 1966–
    The right to bear arms / Michael A. Sommers—1st ed.
      p. cm.
Includes bibliographical references and index.
    ISBN 0-8239-3232-X
    1. Firearms—Law and legislation—United States. 2. Gun control—United States. I. Title.
KF3941 .S66 2000
344.73'0533–dc21

                                    00-010690

Manufactured in the United States of America

About the Author

Michael A. Sommers is a freelance journalist. He is a frequent contributor to *The New York Times, The Globe and Mail,* and *The International Herald Tribune.*

To ALS for many, many things...

Contents

Introduction

"Everyone around me got shot and I begged him for ten minutes not to shoot me. And he just put the gun in my face and started bleeding everywhere and started laughing . . . "

The quote above did not come from a crime novel. Nor was it uttered by a fictional character on a TV cop show or in a big-budget Hollywood movie. The statement was part of a live, unrehearsed, and very real interview of a teenage student by CNN news. The date was April 20, 1999. And tragically, before the day was over, it had already gone down in history as the day of the deadliest school massacre ever to take place in the United States.

It all began at 11:21 AM, on a sunny spring morning in the town of Littleton, Colorado. Dressed in dark trenchcoats, two teenage students stormed into their suburban high school. Armed with shotguns and explosives, they went on a shooting spree that left twelve other students, one teacher, and themselves dead. More than two dozen other people were injured.

The school-shooting massacre in Littleton, Colorado shocked the nation.

The rampage ended only when the two young men turned their guns on themselves. One student, who had been hiding in a closet with a teacher and some friends, said, "I kept thinking to myself, 'This can't be happening to our school.'"

America was shocked by the brutal shootings at Columbine High School. Police, parents, teachers, students, lawmakers, and even the president were forced to re-examine some serious issues about safety, violence, and the role of guns in our lives. What were two teens doing with shotguns? How and where did they get them? Why did they shoot their classmates and teachers before eventually shooting themselves? Could such a shooting have been prevented? If so, how?

This school shooting wasn't a strange occurrence or a one-time fluke. In fact it was the seventh such shooting at an American high school during a span of eighteen months. Worse still, exactly one month after the Colombine massacre,

7

a fifteen-year-old student with two guns opened fire at his high school in Georgia, shooting six of his schoolmates before sticking the gun in his own mouth. Fortunately, nobody was killed. But the fact that a baseball-loving, churchgoing Boy Scout helped himself to his stepfather's collection of fifteen rifles kept America arguing over what to do about guns.

According to the Centers for Disease Control and Prevention (CDC), guns are responsible for more than 38,000 deaths each year in the United States. In 1994 alone, guns were used in 17,800 or 70 percent of all murders. They were also used in more than 18,700 suicides. Furthermore, it is estimated that 135,000 kids take a gun to school with them every day. A 1994 survey of high school students across the nation found that one out of every twenty students carried a gun with them during the last month. Is it any wonder that in 1994, 11,823 young Americans died from gunshot wounds?

These shocking numbers have triggered a lot of debates about guns. Some people think that guns are a problem and that there should be stricter laws that make it more diffi-cult to own, carry, or use such weapons. Some people even believe that guns should be banned altogether. On the other side of the debate are those who think that the responsibility for these violent acts lies not with guns, but with the individ-uals who use them. Such people believe that Americans have the right to protect themselves, their loved ones, and their property—they have the right to "keep and bear arms."

This idea—the right of the people to keep and bear arms—is not just a slogan. It is the central part of the Second Amendment of the United States Constitution. The Second Amendment states:

The Weapon of Choice

In the United States, seven out of ten murders are committed by using guns. Approximately 60 percent are committed with handguns, 5 percent with shotguns, and 3 percent with rifles. In four out of ten robberies, a gun is involved.

"A well regulated Militia, being necessary to the security of a free State, the right of the people to keep and bear Arms, shall not be infringed."

These words were written by the drafters of the United States Constitution more than 200 years ago. One of the ten original amendments that make up the Bill of Rights, the right to bear arms has long been seen as one of the fundamental liberties of every American citizen. But in the last two centuries, America has changed a lot. So have both Americans, and the "arms" they use. Has this changed the way America's politicians, courts of justice, and citizens view this basic American right? That is what we will be exploring in this book.

9

1 A History of Bearing Arms

Today, at the beginning of the twenty-first century, there is no other nation in the Western world in which bearing arms is such a treasured, and hotly debated, Constitutional "right." These days, both Americans and citizens around the world talk of the United States' unique "gun culture." It is impossible to imagine guns not being part of our culture. After all, recent statistics show that there are currently enough arms in America to outfit every man, woman, and child. But guns are not only an important part of our present; they also constitute an important part of our past. Guns have played a significant role in our very unique history. Our use of and attitude towards them have, for better or for worse, shaped who we are as a people and as a nation.

In order to understand who we are today, it is essential to look at the past. More specifically, we need to look at the special group of individuals who created this country after the first thirteen states of the United States of America went to war and won their independence from the King of England. Known as the Founding Fathers, they were the ones who wrote the country's Constitution and Bill of Rights—documents which mapped out how this new and democratic nation would be governed.

In fact, the Constitution and Bill of Rights went beyond simply making up the rules that would govern American citizens. They defined what America would be and what it would become. Since part of that definition included the right to bear arms, we need to look at why arms were so important and what role they played in early American life. However, before we can do that, we need to go even further back in time and trace the origins of the right to bear arms.

As you will see, throughout world history, a citizen's right to bear arms went hand-in-hand with the notions of freedom and democracy.

Ancient Greece and Rome

More than 2,500 years ago, ancient Greece was made up of many independent city-states. Each city functioned as a tiny country, with its own particular type of government. Back then, Athens was one such city-state with a democratic government in which all free citizens met to discuss how Athens should be run. One important right of Athenians was that all free adult men were allowed to bear arms. Naturally, back in 400 BC, there were no guns. Instead, Athenians were permitted to bear arms such as shields, spears, and protective metal armor. By law, upon turning eighteen, all healthy men had to complete two years of military training. This "army" made up the first organized militia of which there are written records. Broadly defined, a "militia" is a group of armed citizens.

Although Athens is known for being a model for modern democracies, you need to realize that only a small percentage of Athenians were actually considered "free" citizens with full rights. Women, foreigners, and slaves (who made up close to one-third of the population) neither participated in government decisions nor shared citizens' rights including the right to bear arms. The one exception to this rule was during times of war, when slaves were temporarily granted citizens' rights and were allowed to carry and use arms.

During the same period, the Roman Empire was in full swing and was thriving. Roman law permitted its citizens to keep arms and use them in self-defense. However, bearing a weapon with intent to kill someone was considered a crime. Of course, as in Athens, not everybody was considered a "Roman citizen." In fact, membership was even more limited than it was in democratic Athens—it was largely restricted to men born into rich and powerful families.

As in Athens, citizens in Rome were trained in using swords, axes, and bows and arrows for defense. As centuries passed, these wealthy arms-bearing Romans dominated the poor unarmed masses who grew increasingly fed up as they watched the nobles live it up in the lap of luxury. Fearing revolt, this rich and powerful minority formed a permanent militia in order to keep the common people under control. Finally however, to keep the masses happy, in the third century BC the Roman government gave in and allowed Roman-born men equal voting rights.

In order to expand its empire, Rome waged many battles to conquer new lands. Unfortunately, over the years,

Philosophers Take Sides

Aristotle

Plato

The right of the individual to own weapons has a long tradition in Western civilization. Legendary Greek philosopher Aristotle thought the bearing of arms was a basic requirement of true citizenship. On the other hand, his teacher, the just-as-famous philosopher Plato, believed that an unarmed population was essential in order to maintain an orderly society.

many battles—and men—were lost. Needing more manpower, like the Athenians before them, Romans hit on the idea of giving some slaves and foreigners citizens' rights. Doing so allowed them to bear arms in the Roman army (and get killed as well).

Europe in the Middle Ages

In the years between 800 to 1100, western Europe was divided into tiny independent regions—nations came later. Each region was centered around a small fortified town or castle ruled by a powerful, wealthy lord. Lords governed through a system known as feudalism.

Under feudalism, a lord who owned land would allow a number of wealthy noblemen and warriors to become his

13

vassals. Being a lord's vassal meant that these noblemen were allowed to farm parts of the lord's land. In return however, vassals had to assemble armies that would fight for the lord and defend his lands if attacked by invaders. These armies were made up of wealthy noblemen called knights. It was the vassals who provided knights with the necessary arms for battle: swords, bows, arrows, helmets, and armor.

Meanwhile, the ones who did the actual farming were the peasants, or common people. Peasants couldn't become vassals or knights and they couldn't bear arms. Instead of getting paid for their work, the vassals guaranteed them protection from invading enemies. This situation began to change in the twelfth century. The brand new kingdom of England was the place where it all began.

Arms in England

Over the decades, England's feudal lords lost their power and their mini-kingdoms were united under a single ruler who became king of all of England. In 1181, England's king was Henry II. Under his rule, a law was passed that was the first to deal with the right to bear arms in the kingdom.

The law, called the Assize of Arms, made it obligatory for all free men (i.e., king's vassals) to possess certain types of arms. The number and type of arms each citizen could possess depended on that citizen's wealth and power. The richer and more important you were, the more arms you could have. The reason behind the Assize was that the king would have a militia ready to fight for him at any time. However, these same weapons provided wealthy people with the potential power to overthrow a bad or overly authoritarian king, should they need to do so.

In 1328, King Edward III signed another important arms law. This law, called the Statute of Northampton, was an ancestor to our contemporary gun control laws in that it made it illegal for people to carry weapons in public places: "No man great or small . . . [shall] go nor ride armed by night nor by day . . . upon pain to forfeit their armor to the King and their bodies to prison at the King's pleasure." Like many of our gun control laws today, the aim of the Statute of Northampton was to reduce the high number of murders and robberies. But (like many of our gun control laws today) while law-abiding citizens obeyed the law, crooks and criminals didn't.

In England, only the rich owned guns. Most kings felt the same as Henry VIII. Henry VIII tried to limit ownership of firearms because his army consisted of commoners who fought with powerful armor-piercing longbows. He thought that if they had access to guns, they would stop practicing with bows and arrows and his army would become weaker. By 1541, however, guns had become mainstream and Henry VIII had to give up his fight and allow widespread ownership and use of most firearms.

Guns became very popular during the civil war that raged between 1642 and 1651, in which the English Parliament rebelled against the abusive authority of King Charles I. A highly organized militia known as the New Model Army was organized by Parliament. Its soldiers were better fed and better paid than any previous army ever had been. They were disciplined and knew how to use guns. Because of this, the New Model Army, led by the popular hero Oliver Cromwell, defeated the king and his army.

Once the king was booted out of power, Cromwell took over the reigns of governing England. Using his great military (and gun) power, he dissolved Parliament and ruled the country as a military dictator. In order to stifle any revolts, he used his New Model Army to keep the English people in line. Often the military force he used was quite brutal. When Cromwell died in 1658, the English were happy to have their king back again. They never forgot how power—backed up by a ruler's strong army—could be easily abused.

In 1671, under Cromwell's royal successor, King Charles II, Parliament passed a "gun control" law called the Game Act. This law prohibited the use of guns, bows, and hunting dogs by anybody—whether rich or poor—who didn't own large areas of land. In effect, only wealthy landowners could hunt and therefore only they had the right to own and bear arms. Coincidentally, these wealthy landowners were the citizens whose power had been increasing the most over the last two centuries. At the same time, the law gave Charles II a nice opportunity to seize the weapons of his potential enemies, thus keeping them disarmed and not dangerous. Other gun control measures imposed by Charles II included a law by which all gunsmiths had to report weekly gun sales, and another by which only those with a license could import weapons into England from abroad.

The English Bill of Rights

The next king in line after Charles II was James II. Although when he came to power in 1685, he promised to "go as far as any man in preserving [England] in all its just rights and

The History of The Gun

Invented in the 1300s, early guns were much more complicated to make than traditional weapons such as swords and spears. It also cost a small fortune to buy one, which put guns out of reach of the poor farmers and peasants.

For a long time, guns were not very well considered. Whereas a sword was a gentleman's weapon, people who used guns were seen as cowards and sinners. In fact, enemy soldiers captured with firearms were frequently killed for using such weapons. But guns were practical and efficient. Kings realized that they were especially useful for winning wars. European rulers who attacked other countries and equipped their armies with firearms were assured a victory. Because of this, some historians credit the invention of the gun with the birth of the modern European nations.

17

liberties," the English quickly caught on that James II intended nothing of the kind. Fuelled by his desire to make Roman Catholicism the most important religion in the country, James II banned all Protestants from bearing arms. Thumbing his nose at the law, he wouldn't let Protestants serve in the army, hold posts in government, or be employed as judges. Anybody who disagreed with him was put on trial. And to enforce his will, he increased the royal army from 5,000 to 30,000 men.

Not surprisingly, James II didn't win any popularity contests with the people. In fact, even most of his own impressive army refused to fight for him. They turned on him, kicking him out of the country in what came to be known as the Glorious (and bloodless) Revolution of 1688.

With James II out of the way, Parliament decided that it was time citizens defended their own rights and liberties. Obviously, leaders such as Oliver Cromwell and James II couldn't be trusted to do it for them. As such, a committee of citizens drew up a declaration called the English Bill of Rights. The rights included in this document ranged from limits on cruel and unusual punishment to freedom of speech for members of Parliament.

The English Bill of Rights also tackled the issue of the right to bear arms. Snubbing James II, the document provided a clause that allowed Protestants to bear arms "for their Defense." It also prevented a ruler from getting too powerful by inserting a clause that declared: "raising or keeping a Standing army within the Kingdom in time of Peace unless it be with Consent of Parliament is against Law."

Sir William Blackstone

Sir William Blackstone (1723-1780) was an English jurist who taught law at Oxford in 1758. Between 1765 and 1769, Blackstone published his lectures, The Commentaries on the Laws of England. This four-volume work was the first attempt to organize centuries of English common law (laws that were accepted through custom or court rulings rather than through actual legislation) into a form that was clear and understandable.

With the Commentaries, Blackstone showed England, and the rest of the world, that British law was just as legitimate as Roman law. The rights and laws he set down—including those concerning the right to bear arms—were a major influence on lawyers and lawmakers in both England and its young colony across the ocean: America.

The English Bill of Rights would prove to be a major inspiration for another Bill of Rights: that of the newly formed United States of America, ratified exactly 100 years later. Many of the rights and liberties set down in the English Bill of Rights, including the right to bear arms, would find their way into the American Bill of Rights.

Of course it is hardly surprising that English law and culture would have such a great impact on the founding of the United States. After all, those who arrived to settle America's thirteen colonies in the early 1600s were mostly British subjects, many of whom had been persecuted for one reason or another. When they traveled across the Atlantic in search of liberty, they brought along their British ideas about militias and guns, rights and rulers, and knowledge of the laws that governed these matters. The big difference however was that the untamed America these settlers encountered was a far cry from the orderly England they had left behind.

2 Guns and the Fight for Freedom in America

The first colonists to arrive in America found themselves in the middle of a vast wilderness. Everything was different. There was no law and no order. People had to fend for and protect themselves. Suddenly guns were more than just for war or for hunting. Guns became a necessary part of life that settlers needed in order to survive.

While in England only the wealthy were given the right to hunt, in colonial America many people had to hunt just so they could have food in their bellies. Some early settlers spent eight to nine months of the year living solely off the meat of the deer they shot. Consequently, most of the land was open to public hunting.

Colonists depended on guns as a means of protection as well. Most of the time, "protection" meant turning the guns on the Native Americans who had inhabited the Americas for thousands of years before Europeans showed up. When the new settlers arrived in America, most Native Americans greeted them warmly. However, after a few decades of the

21

newcomers' attempts to enslave them, steal their land, burn down their homes, and massacre any of them who put up a fight, the Native Americans had had enough.

Many fierce battles ensued. Native Americans attacked colonists with bows, arrows, and spears, and colonists fought back with the muskets they had brought with them from Europe. Even twelve-year-old boys knew how to shoot these muskets and many joined in to help the older men.

The colonists needed all the manpower they could get. The Native Americans were extremely savvy warriors who knew much more about the countryside and its animal inhabitants than did the newcomers. The only thing that kept the colonists from being massacred was their firearms.

Since from the beginning guns played such a key role in everyday colonial American life, owning and using arms was seen as an automatic and natural right. In fact, some of the colonies' governments even insisted upon their citizens being armed. In 1623, Virginia prohibited its residents from travelling unless they were "well armed." In 1658, each Virginia household was obliged to have a working firearm in the house, and in 1673, the colony began actually buying guns for families that couldn't afford them. Meanwhile, in 1644, Massachusetts began fining any citizen who wasn't armed. And in 1770, Georgia passed a law requiring all citizens to take their guns to church with them.

Until the 1760s, the only place you could find a permanent force of British troops was in the colony of New York. This wasn't very reassuring to non-New Yorkers. Realizing that settlers needed to protect themselves, their homes, and their towns, colonial governments had citizens form militias. These militias became the official army in each colony.

They were responsible for keeping order and for defending residents from Native American attackers. To stay in practice, several days out of each year, the men in each militia would get together for military and gun drills. Militias included all white men between the ages of sixteen and sixty. In most cases, each man had to supply his own gun and ammunition. However, some towns kept a common stockpile of arms and ammunition.

Even if guns did seem to be everywhere in colonial America, there did exist certain gun control laws. For example, in many towns it was illegal to hunt or shoot in the streets. It was also considered a crime to use a gun to threaten or scare people. There were also laws about *who* could not and *where* one could not use firearms.

Unsurprisingly, colonists didn't want to encourage the use of guns among Native Americans. A Virginia law prohibited the sale of arms or ammunition to Native Americans while Massachusetts would only let Native Americans carry firearms if they had a license. Another population segment colonists didn't want toting arms were the newly imported African slaves. Frightened of possible slave revolts, both Virginia and Pennsylvania passed laws prohibiting slaves from carrying arms without permission from their masters.

A Revolution in the Making

To us, colonial America might seem as if it was a totally new and free land, far away from England. However, don't forget that it was just that—a colony. And although American realities were very different, American settlers still had to follow rules dictated by the king of England. As time went by, this became more and more of a problem.

Because the thirteen American colonies were English, their citizens were expected to show loyalty to the king of England. Part of this meant paying taxes. However, as England got itself involved in a series of expensive wars, it needed more and more money to pay for military expenses. To raise this money, England looked to its colonies. Consequently, the taxes imposed on the colonies by the English Parliament grew higher and higher.

After about ten years of these increased taxes, American colonists started to get angry. They resented the fact that they had no representation in Parliament and therefore could not protest the constantly increasing taxes. Instead of addressing their concerns, Parliament continued to smother the colonies with new taxes.

As tensions rose, King George III decided to send British troops to Boston to protect English officials who were being threatened by angry colonists. This British army only made the colonists angrier. They felt that the king had no right to station troops in Boston when there was no war being fought. On March 5, 1770, Boston's citizens took to hurling insults, and then rocks, at the British troops. Although the soldiers tried to keep cool, when someone yelled "Fire!" they shot their muskets off into the crowd. Five people were killed in what was soon to be known as the Boston Massacre.

Word of the Boston Massacre spread around the colonies like wild fire. Although they still considered themselves the king's subjects, the colonists resented the British troops. They believed that armies in peacetime were dangerous to a democracy. They believed that a better, more democratic means of defense was to use the people themselves, organized into militias as the colonies had been doing.

Anyone for Tea?

To protest against increasing taxes, some colonists staged a protest in which they dumped forty-five tons of tea from British ships into the Boston harbor.

This protest, known as the Boston Tea Party, angered the British authorities, who responded by closing down the Boston harbor until the spilled tea was paid for. Then they stripped Massachusetts lawmakers of their powers, and replaced them with a new governor named Thomas Gage.

Colonists reacted by dipping British tax collectors in tar and then covering them in feathers. This only reinforced the British view of Americans as savages, criminals, and spoiled brats.

25

The conflicts came to a head in 1775. In September 1774, the First Continental Congress had met in Philadelphia, Pennsylvania. Delegates had decided that until England got rid of its abusive tax laws, the colonies would not trade with their mother country. The king refused to lower taxes. Instead he sent more British troops to squash a new rebellion in Massachusetts.

In Boston, Governor Thomas Gage was ordered to take up arms against the rebels. Against his will (he had lived in the colonies for eighteen years and his wife was American), he did his duty and made plans to take the people's arms and ammunition that had been stored at Concord and Lexington. On April 18, 1775, English troops—called "Redcoats" because of their flaming scarlet uniforms—marched on Concord. Militiamen came out to fight and protect their homes. Suddenly, the Revolution had begun.

The Declaration of Independence and the Fight for Freedom

The Second Continental Congress was held a couple of weeks after the first shot rung out. Delegates called for the people to "bear arms" and fight the Redcoats. However, just fighting was not enough. One of the problems that Congress faced was how to win the revolution. Although the various citizens' militias proved courageous, they lacked the discipline, organization, and experience of the English troops. If America was going to win the war, something had to be done. The solution was to create a Continental army

Rifling Around

During the American Revolution, both sides used muskets and rifles. The advantage of a rifle was that its barrel was fitted with spiral grooves called rifling. After you loaded bullets into the barrel, the rifling put a spin on them when they were fired. Although shooting with a rifle was much more accurate than shooting with a musket, loading one quickly was next to impossible.

that would organize the various colonies' militias under the command of a man named George Washington.

The Congress also urged each colony to set up its own representative government. In doing so, many of these new "states" drew up their own Bill of Rights. Among the rights guaranteed in many of these documents was the right to bear arms. The Virginia Declaration of Rights, for example, went like this: "A well regulated militia, composed of the body of the people, trained to arms, is the proper, natural, and safe defense of a free state." Other states with similar statements were Vermont, Pennsylvania, Massachusetts, and North Carolina.

Only a year into the Revolution, the colonists were already firmly decided that they wanted a definite split from England. The result was the Declaration of Independence, drafted by fifty-six members of the Continental Congress. On July 4, 1776, Congress President John Hancock was the first to sign this historic document. The Declaration of Independence listed many of the colonies' major complaints against the king of England before going on to declare: "These United Colonies are, and of Right ought to be Free and Independent States; that they are Absolved from all Allegiance to the British Crown." When the last of the fifty-six delegates had signed the Declaration, the United States of America was born.

American troops were motivated by their newly declared independence and now, unified as the Continental army, were much more efficient. Nonetheless, the Revolutionary War raged for another five years. Finally however, the British surrendered to General George Washington in October 1781. On September 3, 1783, the Treaty of Paris, signed by both nations, officially granted the United States independence from Great Britain.

3 The Birth of the Second Amendment

Winning the Revolution was a great victory for both the United States of America and for democracy. However, once the treaties had been signed and the soldiers had returned to their homes, some big questions remained to be answered. What kind of new government would this brand new nation have? How much independence would be given to each of the country's thirteen states? What rights and responsibilities could citizens depend upon? And what would be the role of guns?

When the war ended in 1781, the thirteen states were not like the states we know today. Instead, each was like its own little country. States had their own independent governments and Bills of Rights, their own laws, their own militia, and even their own money. And many of them liked it that way—being independent. Although they had banded together to beat the British, once the common enemy was gone, each state was content to go its own way and look out for its own interests. Of course, almost immediately, these

After signing the Declaration of Independence, the members of the Second Continental Congress created the new nation's government.

interests came into conflict with one another. Economic and trade disputes broke out. Some members of the Continental Congress felt that drawing up a federal Constitution would bring together the different states in a strong and harmonious union. If this wasn't possible, it was doubtful whether the new nation could survive.

The Articles of Confederation

In 1776, after drawing up and signing the Declaration of Independence, the members of the Second Continental Congress set to work designing a plan for the new nation's government. The results of this tough task were the Articles of Confederation.

One reason the task was so tough was that many of the future states' delegates refused to approve certain clauses in the document. They were worried about a central or federal government having too much power. Because of this, five years of disputes and debates went by before all thirteen states approved the Articles of Confederation in 1781.

However, by the time all the states had finished with it, the final document had created a federal government with very little power. The national government had no executive branch (a president) and no federal court system. It had no authority to control trade between the states and could only tax the states if they agreed to be taxed. Furthermore, the new government would have no right to form a national army—the states all fiercely opposed this. Each wanted to continue with its own militia. The oppressive years of

English rule had left a bad taste in their mouths. Instead of giving up their power, they wanted citizens to be able to bear arms and fight against any central government that began abusing its power.

The years between 1781 and 1788 proved how insubstantial the Articles of Confederation were. In order to pay debts accumulated from the Revolutionary War, states taxed each other but many of these taxes went unpaid. Rebellions broke out and disputes over trade issues were common. Economically, things became chaotic. Furthermore, Congress soon realized that it couldn't count on state militias to fight federal battles. One of the events that led to this realization was Shays' Rebellion.

In 1786, a Massachusetts farmer named Daniel Shays led a group of several hundred armed men into the state capital of Springfield. Shays and his followers were protesting because the local economy was severely depressed and they were unable to pay off their debts. Because of this, their farms were being taken away from them. The group invaded the state supreme court and forced it to close down. In doing so, they stopped the legal proceedings that were going to take away their farms.

This and other uprisings made some members of Congress nervous. It made them realize that if the nation was to defend itself from armed groups both inside and outside of the country, it would need a stronger and more permanent military force than the local state militias could provide. They concluded that the way things were going, without a stronger federal government and a strong national army, the future of the United States of America was at stake. Hoping to resolve the situation, two members of Congress, James Madison of Virginia and Alexander Hamilton of New York, invited delegates from all of the states to a convention scheduled to begin May 14, 1787, in Philadelphia.

A New Constitution

The weather that spring was so terrible that it took many state delegates a long time to get to Philadelphia. Hence, instead of beginning on May 14, the Constitutional Convention began on May 25. Representatives from twelve states made it to the convention. The one "no show" was rebellious Rhode Island, which liked the Articles of Confederation fine the way they were.

Throughout the long, hot summer of 1787, the fifty-five delegates—later known as the Founding Fathers—met at Independence Hall and debated over how to successfully govern the United States. The delegates began by laying down some ground rules. George Washington, hero of the Revolution, would be their chairman. Each state would have one vote and only one vote. And everything discussed at the convention was top secret. The press was kept in the dark. Security guards were hired to chase away spies and eavesdroppers. Delegates were not even allowed to write home to talk about what was going on. Although some delegates got fed up and left, most stuck around to help write the new Constitution that became the country's bible. The Constitution that they finally hammered out is the same one we still use today.

Among the many decisions the Founding Fathers made was how to organize the new federal government. Power would be shared between an executive branch (the president), a legislative branch (Congress), and a judicial branch (the courts). Such a division ensured that no one branch could become too powerful and abuse the people's rights. If one branch got out of hand, there were always the other two branches to keep it in line. This system came to be known as one of "checks and balances."

Congress was made up of two houses. One house, called the House of Representatives, would have representatives from all states. The number of representatives would be based on the state's population. Virginia, for instance, being one of the most populated states at the time, had more representatives than the less populated state of New Jersey. The other house, called the Senate, would have an equal number of representatives from each state. In other words, both Virginia, New Jersey (which had a small population), and every other state would each send two senators to Congress. Congress' powers would include passing laws, raising taxes, regulating the national economy, and declaring war. It could raise and support an army or navy, and summon state militias to defend against rebellions and invasions.

The president's job was to carry out the laws Congress passed, make decisions about foreign affairs, and command the military. Meanwhile it was up to the federal courts to reject laws passed by Congress or the state governments that federal judges believed were contrary to laws or rights set down in the Constitution.

In the same way that power was balanced between executive, legislative, and judicial branches, it was also divided between the federal government and the state governments. Some of the Founding Fathers, known as Federalists,

Who Were the Founding Fathers?

The fifty-five so-called "Founding Fathers"—the men who created the United States—were a diverse bunch. The youngest "Father" was twenty-six-year-old Jonathan Dayton. The oldest "Father," Benjamin Franklin, was eighty-one. When he signed the Constitution, he was so frail that he needed help holding his pen. Other famous Fathers included George Washington, James Madison, George Mason, and Alexander Hamilton. Most had been to university. At the same time, they practiced a wide range of professions: from commerce and farming to law and medicine. Most had fought during the Revolution and many held political posts in their home states.

35

believed that a strong federal government was necessary to bind the country together. Because of their arguments, the Constitution put the federal government in charge of the national economy, relations with foreign countries, and military affairs. Other Founding Fathers were worried about the states losing too much autonomy. These Anti-Federalists felt that in many cases the states themselves knew best about certain local issues. Their positions were reflected in a Constitution that decided to let states run their own economies, organize and train their own militias, and make many of their own laws.

Signing the Constitution— A Difficult Task

Getting the Constitution signed by all the delegates proved to be a difficult process. The biggest stumbling block was the Anti-Federalists. Many feared that the Constitution gave too much power to the federal government at the states' expense. They feared that such a government might abuse the peoples' rights just as the English government had. Anti-Federalist Founding Father George Mason of Virginia said that he would sooner chop off his right hand than use it to sign the Constitution.

Other Anti-Federalists agreed with him. What many wanted was a Bill of Rights that would safeguard the rights and liberties of the citizens and the states. Although he was in France at the time (serving as ambassador), Thomas Jefferson, author of the Declaration of Independence and future third president, wrote a letter to his friend and

Founding Father James Madison, in which he said: "A bill of rights is what the people are entitled to against every government on earth."

Although Federalists thought that the Constitution was fine as it was, they realized that without a Bill of Rights, the Anti-Federalist delegates wouldn't sign it and the states wouldn't accept it. For this reason, they agreed to support a Bill of Rights that would be added to the Constitution at a later date. With this assurance, on September 17, 1787, thirty-nine delegates approved the new Constitution. Thirteen others had already gone home and only three delegates refused to sign at all. One of these was Anti-Federalist George Mason.

Of course, the Constitutional battle was far from being over. Although the delegates had approved it, the Constitution had to be ratified, or approved, by at least nine out of thirteen states before being adopted as the law of the land.

Founding Fathers James Madison, Alexander Hamilton, and John Jay wrote arguments in support of the Constitution. Called the "Federalist Papers," these were published in the country's main newspapers in an attempt to get state support for the Constitution. Echoing the Anti-Federalists' arguments, many states were afraid that the Constitution gave too much power to the federal government. They wanted guarantees that protected citizens' basic rights and liberties, such as the right to free speech and the right to free press. One of the most important freedoms that they felt the Constitution didn't address was the individual's right to bear arms. The writers of the Constitution argued that ownership and use of guns was such a natural part of American life that it was taken for granted that the people could keep and bear arms. However, individual states, many of whose governments possessed a Bill of Rights that specifically upheld their citizens' right to bear arms, wanted this and other rights to be set down in black and white.

Once assurances were made that the right to bear arms and other fundamental individual liberties would be included in a Bill of Rights that would be amended, or added, to the Constitution, the states eventually came around one by one. Although they had fought for a clause stating that "Congress shall never disarm any citizen, unless such as are or have been in actual rebellion," Delaware was the first of the thirteen states to ratify the Constitution. Even though many states had similar amendments concerning the right to bear arms, almost all of them approved the Constitution as well. (The two hold-outs were North Carolina and Rhode Island. North Carolina ratified the Constitution in November of 1789 and Rhode Island in May of 1790). Amidst much celebrating, in June 1788, the Constitution became the law of the land.

The Bill of Rights and the Second Amendment

No sooner had the festivities died down than the Founding Fathers were back at the drawing board. This time they went to work creating the Bill of Rights they had promised to the Anti-Federalists and the states. James Madison was the one who actually did most of the writing of the amendments to the Constitution. He originally penned seventeen, but these were whittled down to the ten amendments that were accepted and which still exist today.

Constitutional Curiosities

• At 4,400 words, the U.S. Constitution is the shortest constitution of any country in the world.

• When the Constitution was signed, the population of the United States was four million. Today it is more than 280 million.

• The Constitution was actually "penned" by a Pennsylvania clerk named Jacob Shallus. He was paid $30 for his efforts (today's equivalent would be around $264).

• Since 1952, the Constitution has been housed in the National Archives Building in Washington, DC. During the day, pages one and four are displayed in a bulletproof case. The case contains helium and water vapor to preserve the paper. At night, the pages are lowered into a vault, behind five-ton doors that can survive a nuclear explosion.

Among the rights the Bill of Rights guaranteed were free speech; freedom of the press; freedom to practice all religions; freedom to meet in public; freedom against unreasonable searches and seizures in one's home; the right to a speedy, public trial by jury; the right to an attorney when accused of a crime; the right to reasonable bail; no cruel or unusual punishment; and no requirement to house soldiers in one's home during peace time. The states were satisfied by the Tenth Amendment which automatically assured them power over all matters not granted to the federal government in the Constitution. And everybody seemed satisfied by the Second Amendment concerning the right to bear arms.

Madison labored a long time over the wording of the Second Amendment. Seeking inspiration, he turned to the English Bill of Rights of 1689 as well as looking at many of the early Bills of Rights written by the individual American colonies. Many of these state Bills of Rights granted the people as a whole the right to bear arms for the defense of the state and recognized the right of individual citizens to bear arms. However, the two Declarations of Rights that influenced Madison the most were Virginia's and Pennsylvania's.

Written by George Mason in 1776, Virginia's Declaration of Rights stated: "That a well-regulated militia, composed of the body of the people, trained to arms, is the proper, natural and safe defense of a free State; that standing armies, in time of peace, should be avoided, as dangerous to liberty.

Penned the same year, the Pennsylvania Declaration of Rights declared: "That the people have a right to bear arms for the defense of themselves and the state; and as standing armies in the time of peace are dangerous to liberty, they ought not to be kept up."

James Madison

James "Jemmy" Madison (1751-1836) stood five feet, four inches and weighed less than 100 pounds—too small to serve in the Revolutionary War. Nevertheless, he was a heavyweight in other ways. At twenty-five, he helped draft the constitution for Virginia before moving onto the U.S. Constitution.

With his wife Dolley Todd at his side, Madison was elected president in 1809 and remained undefeated until 1817. Although his presidency floundered when British troops stormed the capital in 1812, Dolley Madison's popularity soared when she snuck out of the White House, determined that the British would not be able to get their hands on crucial government documents and a portrait of George Washington.

James Madison was the last of the Founding Fathers to pass away. When he died in 1836, he was eighty-two years old.

From these models, Madison came up with the following rough draft of the Second Amendment:

*"The right of the people to keep and bear arms shall not
be infringed; a well armed and well regulated militia being
the best security of a free country: but no person religious-
ly scrupulous of bearing arms shall be compelled to render
military service in person."*

He submitted this draft to Congress where its wording
was much discussed. Eventually the amendment was
approved, but the final clause about religious scruples was
removed. This is because some members of Congress
believe it gave some people an excuse to avoid military service. In the end, the Second Amendment consisted of
twenty-seven words:

*"A well regulated Militia, being necessary to the security
of a free State, the right of the people to keep and bear
Arms, shall not be infringed."*

On September 25, 1789, this and eleven other
Amendments were adopted by Congress. By December 15,
1791, the necessary number of states had ratified ten of
these Amendments. These ten, including the Second
Amendment, became the United States Bill of Rights.

4 Guns In America During the 1800s

The United States of America entered the nineteenth century as a free country, its citizens proud and protective of their hard won liberties. As you know, one of these liberties was the people's right to bear arms. In fact, the people had won these liberties *because* they bore arms. So you can imagine how important this right was to early Americans as they set to work building a new nation.

All for Guns and Guns for All

Although it is hard to imagine, you must remember that in 1800, the United States was a much smaller, weaker, and less wealthy nation than it is today. And don't forget that most of the Midwest and the western states were still largely undiscovered and unsettled.

43

In the early years of the nineteenth century, French Emperor Napoleon Bonaparte was hard at war, invading and adding various European countries to his empire. Fearful that Napoleon's imperial dreams might cause him to cross the Atlantic, nervous American gun manufacturers started increasing the production of guns.

Not only did the quantity of firearms manufactured increase, but the quality did as well. In fact, by the middle of the century, American military arms were considered to be the best in the world. American manufacturers were exporting their wares to countries all over the world. Meanwhile at home, as guns became more available and more affordable, Americans were buying up guns like never before.

Throughout the nineteenth century guns remained a central part of American culture. Hunting and target shooting were the most popular outdoor sports. And dueling was the fashionable way to resolve any argument.

Then, of course, there was the West to be won. The nineteenth century marked America's great expansion across the plains to the Pacific. To the pioneers and settlers who journeyed west, guns were as essential as they had been to the first colonists who arrived in the New World. Guns put food on the table. They also allowed settlers to protect themselves from Native American attackers.

The native peoples were not pleased at having newcomers seize their lands and horn in on their hunting grounds. They put up a fight, meaning that ambushes, battles, and massacres between settlers and Native Americans became commonplace throughout the American West. The conflicts only came to a halt in 1890, with the defeat of Chief Big

Eli Whitney

One man was largely responsible for a revolution in gun manufacturing. His name was Eli Whitney (1765-1825). And before this Yale graduate turned his attention to manufacturing arms, he had just finished inventing the cotton gin. The cotton gin was a machine that cleaned the seeds out of freshly picked cotton. This machine would make the South prosperous and Whitney himself rich.

Before Eli Whitney came along, every gun bought, and shot, was different. The reason for this was that each gun was put together out of a series of hand-made parts. Since no two parts were exactly the same, each part would only fit other parts of the same gun. If one part broke, the whole gun was pretty much useless.

Whitney's idea was to have machines produce gun parts instead of humans doing so. This way each would be identical and interchangeable. Manufacturers would also be able to produce many more arms.

To prove his point, Whitney opened up his own factory. After a couple of start-up problems, he was producing arms that were of a better quality than those that were handmade. In fact, Whitney became the most important manufacturer of arms in the country. In the meantime, he succeeded in single-handedly jumpstarting the industrial revolution in the northern United States.

Foot and the last free tribe of Lakotas at the Battle of Wounded Knee, in South Dakota.

In 1849, the discovery of gold in California drew thousands and thousands of settlers to the West. Knowing how important guns would be to their survival, Congress went as far as to pass an 1849 law that provided free army weapons to the new residents of California, Oregon, and New Mexico. In doing so, the government endorsed the individual's right to bear arms. Congress knew that without any police or militia to protect them, each citizen would have to look out for himself.

As a result, guns and gun culture became part and parcel of the Far West experience. Wearing a loaded gun in the street was just like donning a hat and putting on a pair of boots. As the century wore on and small towns sprung up, local governments tried to enforce some law and order in an attempt to prevent the many public shootouts that had become commonplace. However, the typical response was not unlike that of a small Texas frontier town. When law officials posted notices that prohibited carrying guns, the local boys promptly shot holes through the notices. For a long time in fact, life in the West was just like in the westerns. How fast you could draw was more important than the law.

Meanwhile, back east the situation was much different. A far cry from an untamed wilderness, the eastern states were rapidly urbanizing. Cities were growing at an accelerated rate. Nobody needed to hunt much of anything and most of the Native Americans were dead or had gone elsewhere. This made it pretty pointless to haul around a big rifle. The only guns that were sometimes

Death by Dueling

Alexander Hamilton (1755-1804), one of the more influential Founding Fathers, was one of the authors of the Federalist Papers. It is his face that is etched onto $10 bills.

When Hamilton was fifteen, his father went bankrupt. This forced young Alexander to go to work in a counting house. His math must have been good because when his friend George Washington became president, he made Hamilton secretary of the treasury. This was generous of Washington, considering that before his election, Hamilton was one of a group of politicians who felt that the U.S. would be better off with a king. Hamilton had even drafted a letter to Prussia's Prince Henry asking the prince if he wanted the job.

In 1800, when Thomas Jefferson ran for president, he tied with another candidate named Aaron Burr. The tie was to be broken by the House of Representatives, whose leader was Hamilton. Hamilton convinced his colleagues to choose Jefferson over Burr. Then shortly after, when Burr campaigned for governor of New York, Hamilton again coaxed voters not to side with Burr. By this time Burr was not happy. He challenged Hamilton to a duel with guns and fatally wounded him.

Although Americans mourned the loss of this Founding Father, they had no problem with private citizens owning, carrying, and sorting out their affairs with dueling pistols.

carried were small pistols or revolvers. Known as "hand guns" these were used for self-protection and were kept hidden from view. In general however, most eastern city residents didn't walk around with guns.

The firearms that were used in the East were being used increasingly by criminals. As more and more people moved to industrializing cities, there was a surge of violence and crime, riots and strikes. The fact that crooks and mobs took to using guns made American cities dangerous places and made American citizens fearful of guns ending up in the wrong hands. A few citizens began calling for some type of gun control so that they could walk the streets safely.

The Have-Nots

Whether you lived in the Wild West or in the urban East, throughout the nineteenth century every American citizen had the right to bear arms. As we have seen, most American citizens took full advantage of this right. And they had the full support of local, state, and federal governments to do so.

Of course, there were those who didn't have such rights because they weren't considered U.S. citizens. Although America was supposedly a democracy, democratic liberties were not extended to either African Americans or Native Americans. In terms of African Americans, this view became official on March 6, 1857. On this date, the U.S. Supreme Court ruled that blacks, whether free or slaves, were not entitled to the rights set down in the Constitution and Bill of Rights. Known as the Dred Scott case, this ruling by the judicial branch of the

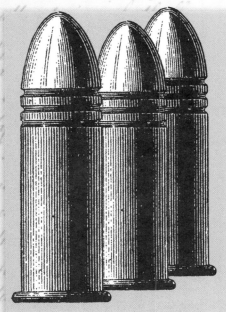

Guns in the 1800s

Guns used in the nineteenth century ranged from muskets and rifles to pistols and shotguns. By the end of the century, America's gunmakers had invented the automatic and semiautomatic guns. These could fire a series of bullets in rapid succession when the trigger was held down. With these innovations, guns became even more efficient—and more deadly.

federal government made it clear that blacks had "no rights which any white man was bound to respect." Such rights included the right to bear arms.

Interestingly, although blacks were forbidden from owning and carrying arms, the federal government was happy to make an exception when the Civil War broke out in 1861. In the North, at first only white volunteers were allowed to join the Union army. However, when not enough white men volunteered, Congress passed the Militia Act of July 1862. The act required all males between eighteen and forty-five to fight for the Union. This included black males as well, who formed their own regiments. All in all, over 200,000 black Americans fought for the Union during the Civil War. Of these,

This Union infantry corporal is holding a pocket revolver. Black people were forbidden from owning and carrying arms until the Civil War, when black men were drafted into the Union army.

38,000 lost their lives. As its losses grew, even the Confederate South was ready to let slaves do some fighting. But by the time a Confederate law had been passed that allowed blacks to fight, it was too late. The Union had already won the war. Some believe that the Yankees' victory was partly due to the added manpower and fighting skills of the black soldiers.

Of course, one of the good things to come out of the end of the Civil War was the end of slavery. In 1865, the Thirteenth Amendment was passed, prohibiting all forms of slavery in the United States. This was followed by the passing of the Civil Rights Act in 1866. The Civil Rights Act was the first law to declare that "all persons born in the United States and not subject to any foreign power" were American citizens. As such, these citizens "of every race and color" could enjoy the "full and equal benefit of all laws and proceedings for the security of person and property, as is enjoyed by white citizens."

The federal government had recognized that, in terms of black Americans, such rights—including the right to bear arms—were necessary. Whether they were free or not, blacks needed to protect themselves. Even after the Civil War and the passing of the Civil Rights Act, black Americans were often lynched, hanged, shot, or burned by angry white mobs—for the most part Southerners. Instead of coming to their defense, white militias in the South were often responsible for such racist attacks. Frederick Douglass, the former slave who was one of the great leaders in the fight to end slavery, publicly encouraged black Americans to own and use guns to defend themselves.

In spite of the Civil Rights Act—which in 1866 officially became a part of the Constitution when its contents were ratified as the Fourteenth Amendment—the white militias of many Southern states continued to invade black homes and seize their guns. Furthermore, governments of many Southern states passed state laws known as "black codes" that prohibited blacks from keeping or carrying any type of firearm.

The states argued that the Bill of Rights applied only to laws passed by the federal government, and not to the states. This view was upheld by the Supreme Court in 1876 when a case known as *The United States vs. Cruikshank* was heard. The case questioned whether it was constitutional to prevent blacks from legally bearing arms. The Court's interpretation was that such questions were up to individual states, not the federal government. Until the court changed its interpretation, in many states black Americans would not be allowed to own or use guns until well into the early twentieth century.

Other "have-nots" were Native Americans. In 1835, President Andrew Jackson began a national policy of expelling Native Americans from their lands in the East and giving the land to newly arrived white settlers. Native Americans were herded out West onto plots of lands called reservations. In return for moving, the government equipped the Native Americans with "arms, ammunition, and other indispensable items." They were supplied with steel and iron and taught to be gunsmiths.

Of course, as Native Americans became increasingly armed, settlers out West became increasingly unhappy. They still feared attacks from their traditional enemies. As a

In the nineteenth century, Native Americans were prohibited from owning guns, and were not extended the same rights to bear arms as other citizens until 1979.

result of such complaints, Congress passed a law in 1876 banning the sale of certain types of ammunition to "hostile Indians" in certain western states. Obviously, without ammunition Native Americans couldn't use most of the guns being manufactured at the time. Things became more difficult after the Supreme Court, in 1884, ruled that Native Americans, even those who left their tribes and lived with whites, were not American citizens and therefore could not bear arms. In fact, Native Americans would have to wait until 1924 before they officially became U.S. citizens and until 1979 before they received the same rights to bear arms as other Americans.

In the twentieth century, cities grew quickly, and guns began to play a large role in urban violence.

5 The Twentieth Century: Guns and Gun Laws

It would be safe to say that prior to the twentieth century, life in America was probably a lot simpler. The United States was a smaller country with a smaller population. There was less technology, less diversity, and less complexity. There were not as many options and there were fewer choices to make.

The twentieth century brought with it many changes. And these changes had great effects on American society and culture. They also had a great effect on how Americans used and viewed guns. By the end of the 1800s, the final frontier had been tamed and industrialization was the name of the game. People no longer needed guns in order to survive, but the large number of guns being produced were more accurate and sophisticated than ever before. In the many new and quickly growing cities, the birth of organized police forces meant that citizens no longer had to rely on guns to protect themselves. They certainly didn't need guns to kill deer for dinner or shoot Native Americans. What then were guns being used for?

Increasingly, they were being used for purposes that were less essential and more destructive. In the rapidly expanding cities, economic depression and unemployment led to strikes, riots, and criminal activity.

Unfortunately, guns played a big part in this new urban violence. More and more, guns were used to kill and maim, not just to defend one's person, property, or country. In fact, the entire country went into shock when President William McKinley was assassinated by a deranged anarchist in 1901. This event was a sign of things to come throughout the rest of the century. The result was that frightened Americans, confronted with daily hold-ups and shoot-outs in the streets, began thinking twice about the right to bear arms. If nobody disputed the actual right, people criticized the easy availability of these dangerous weapons.

The changes in American society and in the role of guns in this society would not only affect the views of private citizens, but those of federal and state governments, lawmakers and courts. Throughout the nineteenth century nobody challenged either the Second Amendment or the people's unlimited right to bear arms. However, in the twentieth century, interpretation of this fundamental liberty would become a major source of debate between those who believed gun control was necessary and their opponents who felt that gun control infringed upon the sacred Constitutional rights spelled out in the Second Amendment.

The First Gun Control Laws

Public concern over gun-related violence at the beginning of the century quickly led to the creation of the first gun

Women and Guns

In 1902, Smith and Wesson manufactured the Lady Smith revolver, the first gun specifically designed for a woman's hand. The Lady Smith was made until 1921. The company halted production when they discovered that it had become the favorite weapon of prostitutes.

Women today own more guns than women 100 years ago. An estimated 15 million women legally own firearms. Most women buy guns for self-defense.

control laws. Various state governments felt that it was necessary to regulate or prohibit ownership and use of certain types of arms as a measure of public safety. For example, in 1907, Texas placed a large tax on gun merchants that made it more expensive to buy arms.

In 1913, Oregon passed a law prohibiting anyone without a license from purchasing a handgun. And in 1911, a much-hyped string of shootings in New York City led the state of New York to pass a law that made it a serious crime, or felony, to carry, or even keep, any concealed firearm without a permit. Known as the Sullivan Law, this was the first time in American history that a law regulated not only the right to carry firearms, but the right to buy and keep them as well. When police started arresting people with guns that were all of a sudden illegal, many people protested (unsuccessfully) that their fundamental rights, guaranteed by the Second Amendment, were being abused. Nonetheless, by the end of the 1920s, seventeen other states had passed similar gun control laws.

Meanwhile, around the country, it seemed that violent crime and strikes pitting gun-toting workers, bosses, and police against each other were out of control. In 1919, the first federal attempt at regulating gun ownership occurred with the passage of the War Revenue Act. To pay off federal debts racked up during World War I, the act placed a 10 percent tax on the sale of firearms. Although this law was a small measure, it was only the beginning. During the 1920s, hundreds of laws regulating the sale and ownership of guns were introduced into Congress. Although most didn't get too far, one that did was the Miller Bill.

During the 1920s and 1930s, crime grew much worse in the United States. Prohibition—which made the production, sale, and consumption of all alcohol illegal—was responsible for creating a dangerous underground world of illegal liquor activities.

Then came the Depression, in which one out of four Americans was unemployed, poor, and desperate. Gun-related violence was worse than ever before as gangsters like Al Capone took to using brutal new weapons such as sawed-off shotguns, silencers, and machine guns. Since there was no reason any law-abiding citizen would ever need to bear such arms, terrorized Americans demanded that the government do something about these "gangster weapons."

In response to this public outcry, Congress passed the National Firearms Act on June 26, 1934. This was the first federal law ever passed by Congress that actually restricted the

The Miller Bill

Introduced by House Representative John F. Miller of Washington, the Miller Bill proposed to illegalize private citizens' ability to buy concealable guns through the U.S. mail. The bills' supporters felt that such a law was necessary in order to help prevent the flow of firearms to states that had passed their own gun control laws. Those who opposed the bill felt that such a law was unconstitutional because it would limit the personal rights of American citizens guaranteed in the Second Amendment.

One of the biggest opponents of the bill was Texas Congressman Thomas Blanton, who had this to say:

> "I hope that every American boy, whether he is from Texas, New York, or Washington, will know how to use a six-shooter . . . I hope every woman in America will learn how to use a revolver. I hope she will not use it but I hope she will know how. It will be for her safety; it will safeguard her rights . . . That is what the framers of this Constitution had in mind when they said the Congress should never infringe upon the right to keep firearms in the home."

In spite of his arguments, the Miller Bill became law in 1927.

keeping and bearing of arms. Fearing that the Supreme Court would rule that an actual federal gun control law was unconstitutional under the Second Amendment, the law was proposed as part of a tax bill aimed at taxing the sale of certain firearms. By placing a $200 tax and a registration requirement on the "gangster weapons" mentioned above, the government hoped to make it very difficult for private citizens to own such guns. Furthermore, makers, importers, and dealers of guns would have to pay registration fees to the federal treasury for such weapons, as well as keeping records of their sales.

The follow-up to this law was the Federal Firearms Act of 1938. This act obliged all makers and dealers of firearms to have a license. It also prohibited guns from being sold from one state to another and made it illegal to sell guns to criminals and to those charged with having committed a crime. Overall, the Federal Firearms Act gave the federal government even more power to regulate the sale and possession of guns. In doing so, it revealed the government's belief that restricting sale and ownership of guns did not conflict with the Second Amendment's right to bear arms.

Guns in America after World War II

Although World War II broke out in 1939, the United States only entered the war when the Japanese bombed Pearl Harbor, Hawaii, on December 7, 1941. With such an enormous demand for arms worldwide, the American weapons industry was cranking out more arms than ever before. Though the war ended in 1945, America's weapons industry actually stepped

Why Do Criminals Prefer Guns?

Guns give criminals many advantages:

* The criminal can stay far away from his or her victim, so the victim is less able to fight back.
* It is easier to shoot someone than stick a knife into him or her.
* It is easier to control many people at the same time with a gun.
* People are less likely to run away when faced with a gun.

up arms production once peace had been declared. After all, during the war years plants had expanded, jobs had been created, and big money was being made. Nobody wanted the boom to stop. Even the federal government was making money selling surplus weapons after the war.

American soldiers who came back from fighting, returned home with their guns, their military training, and a keen interest in all types of weapons. Guns were a symbol of victory, of freedom and democracy. Throughout the late 1940s and early 1950s, gun culture flourished in America like never before.

All of this changed, however, one bright sunny morning in Dallas, Texas. The date was November 22, 1963. And as the young and popular President John F. Kennedy rode by the crowds in his open car, his wife Jackie beside him, a man named Lee Harvey Oswald gunned him down.

In Dallas, Texas, on the morning of November 22, 1963, President John F. Kennedy was fatally shot.

The entire nation was shocked by this brutal assassination. Many have since said that it was the day America lost its innocence. The assassination, captured on film, deeply shocked Americans. The whole nation was suddenly confronted with some negative aspects of its gun culture, specifically the tragic consequences of uncontrolled ownership and use of arms. The fact that Oswald had purchased his Italian rifle from a mail-order catalogue enraged many Americans. They felt that there ought to be more control over who owned guns and how they got them in the first place. A week after President Kennedy's death, close to twenty gun control bills had been introduced in Congress. And a major debate was being waged over the true meaning of the Second Amendment. On one hand, there were those who supported gun control. Their interpretation of the Second Amendment followed that of House Representative John Lindsay of New York:

> *"Today the Nation no longer depends on the citizen's weapon, nor does the citizen himself. And, most significant, the population is now densely packed into urban areas, and it is diverse and mobile. In our changed and complicated society, guns have become more dangerous, and they demand more careful use. The Constitution must be interpreted in the light of the times; protection today means the reasonable regulation of firearms—not the absence of regulation."*

On the other hand were those who opposed gun control. They felt that such measures threatened the basic individual liberties set out by the Founding Fathers in the Constitution. Their interpretation of the Second Amendment was summed up by Congressman John J. Flynt Jr.:

The Right to Bear Arms

"One of the prized possessions of Americans has been the right to own and possess firearms and to use these firearms in defense of country, in defense of home, in self-defense, provided that use is done in a legal and legitimate manner. The attitude toward firearms has become a historical tradition in the United States. I think it is safe to say that it represents a priceless freedom won by those preceding us as Americans, which few if any other nations enjoy."

Although these gun control bills generated a lot of debate, none of them ultimately became laws due to the strong arguments of those who opposed any form of gun regulation. However, throughout the 1960s, opinion polls showed that over 70 percent of Americans supported stricter gun control laws. While the federal government was loath to react to these figures, between 1965 and 1968, many state governments did pass gun laws. Particularly strict ones were passed in cities such as New York, Chicago, and Philadelphia.

In 1968, two more assassinations of important public figures once again rocked the nation. On April 4, beloved civil rights leader Dr. Martin Luther King, Jr. was gunned down with a rifle on the balcony of his motel room in Memphis, Tennessee. Shortly after, on June 5, presidential candidate Robert F. Kennedy (younger brother of John) was killed by a pistol in a Los Angeles hotel.

This time, Congress quickly passed the Gun Control Act of 1968. Replacing the Federal Firearms Act of 1938, this law placed more restrictions on sales of guns between states (handguns, for instance, could not be purchased out of state) and required all gun dealers to keep records of the people to whom they sold weapons in case the police

Malcolm X and the Black Power Movement

Malcolm X was a Muslim minister and African American leader of a movement whose aim was to unite black people all over the world.

The 1950s and 1960s were turbulent times for civil rights activists in the United States. Although courts ruled that blacks were equal to whites, and that the two races should be provided with the same rights, liberties, and protection under the law, many racist whites were threatened by these rulings. They took out their fear in violent ways, by beating and even murdering both African Americans and civil rights workers.

Malcolm X responded to this racism by preaching to African Americans, instilling in them a strong sense of black pride. In the face of the violence inflicted upon them, Malcolm X urged black Americans to use their constitutional rights as free American citizens to bear arms in self-defense:

"The Constitution of the United States of America clearly affirms the right of every American citizen to bear arms. And as Americans, we will not give up a single right guaranteed under the Constitution . . . We assert that in those areas where the government is either unable or unwilling to protect the lives and property of our people, that our people are within their rights to protect themselves by whatever means necessary."

On February 21, 1965, Malcolm X was assassinated.

wanted to check on them. It prohibited all sales of guns through the mail as well as all sales of rifles, shotguns, and ammunition to minors under the age of eighteen. Certain people, such as felons and the mentally ill, were prohibited from owning firearms. Those who could buy guns had to sign a statement saying that they were qualified to do so. Finally, those who violated any of the above conditions could have their guns automatically taken away from them.

In order to avoid accusations that the law was contrary to the Second Amendment, the Gun Control Act of 1968 took care to state that its true aim was to help cut down on crime and violence. The Act had no intention of "discouraging or eliminating the private ownership or use of firearms by law-abiding citizens for lawful purposes... [such as] hunting, trapshooting, target shooting, personal protection, or any other lawful activity." In spite of such assurances, gun control opponents were unhappy due to what they viewed as the biggest federal restriction ever on the rights of American gunowners.

Even with the Gun Control Act of 1968 in place, gun-related crimes and violence in the United States only escalated throughout the 1960s and 1970s. And even though many other gun control laws were proposed to Congress— in 1976 alone, there were more than 200 bills dealing with some form of federal gun control—those who opposed gun control were increasingly influential. This became apparent in 1981. On March 31 of that year, President Ronald Reagan was shot in the chest by a bullet from a cheap, poorly made handgun known as a "Saturday night special." Although nobody was killed, the president and three other people were wounded. Injured the worst was the president's press secretary, James S. Brady. A shot in the head led to Brady being permanently brain damaged.

In response to this shooting, a handgun crime control bill was introduced into Congress. It prohibited the sale of Saturday night specials and enforced a twenty-one-day wait on any handgun purchases. Pawnshops could not sell guns and anyone convicted of a serious crime committed with a handgun would have to serve a minimum jail sentence of five years. Even with the population up in arms over increased gun-related violence, gun control opponents such as the National Rifle Association fought hard against the bill. In the end, the bill didn't even make it to the voting stage.

In fact, restrictions on gun ownership were actually reduced the next time Congress passed a law related to guns. The 1986 Firearms Owners' Protection Act made it even easier to own a gun. Overturning previous restrictions, it was now possible to purchase a rifle or shotgun in another state and through the mail. It once again became possible to carry (unloaded) weapons from one state to another. Gun dealers didn't have to do as much record keeping of sales as they had before. And a gun could no longer be taken from its owner without a court hearing. The National Rifle Association hailed this new law as "the most historic piece of pro-gun regulation ever enacted."

Nonetheless, as the twentieth century came to a close, Congress did pass some significant gun control laws. In 1986, it became a crime for any individual to own a machine gun (those who had purchased theirs before 1986 could hold on to them, however). It also became illegal to sell or use "cop-killer" bullets. Ordinary bullets are made from lead. Cop-killer bullets are made from harder metals such as steel, brass, iron, bronze, or copper. Although lead bullets can't puncture the bulletproof vests worn by police officers, these cop-killer bullets can.

In 1989, Patrick Purdy opened fire on a Stockton, California elementary school playground with an assault rifle. This shooting spree ended with five children murdered and twenty-nine others wounded. Shocked Americans, particularly parents, were increasingly upset by instances of gun violence on school grounds. Purdy's attack had been the fifth instance of a school shooting in one year. Following this tragic shooting, several states passed laws banning semi-automatic assault weapons. And in 1994, Congress did the same when it passed the Violent Crime Control and Law Enforcement Act. This law banned both the manufacture and ownership of semi-automatic rifles, handguns or shotguns (although exceptions were made for a few semi-automatic rifles used by hunters).

At the same time, gun culture and gun violence wasn't only invading the nation's schools. It was also becoming a big problem in private homes across America. As families splintered and an increasingly fast-paced life increased emotional stress on family members, incidents of domestic violence seemed to increase. And more and more, violence between a husband and his wife, a girlfriend and her boyfriend, a parent and his or her kids, came to a fatal head due to the presence of a gun in the home.

The Menendez Brothers

One of the most talked-about and shocking examples of a family torn apart by guns was the 1989 Menendez murders. On

The Brady Bill

After his tragic shooting injury, James Brady and his wife Sarah decided to take action against what they saw as out-of-control gun violence in America. They formed a group called Handgun Control Inc. and drafted the so-called Brady Bill, which proposed a seven-day waiting period on all handgun purchases. Such a waiting period would allow police to make background checks on applicants. If the applicant turned out to have a criminal record or a history of mental illness for example, the sale would not go through. Every year, for more than ten years, the Brady Bill was introduced to Congress and voted upon. Every year, for more than ten years, it was defeated by gun control opponents.

Finally, in 1993, voters in Congress passed the bill which subsequently became the Brady Act. Even though the waiting period had been reduced to five days, those who supported it believed that it would stop criminals from buying guns as well as reduce "crimes of passion" committed in the heat of the moment.

the evening of August 20, 1989, Jose and Kitty Menendez were lounging in the family room of their $4 million, twenty-three-room mansion in Beverly Hills watching a James Bond video called *The Spy Who Loved Me*. The couple's two sons, twenty-one-year-old Lyle and eighteen-year-old Eric, had gone out.

At around 10 PM, a car drove up in front of the Menendez mansion and two men got out. Although the house—formerly rented by the likes of Prince and Elton John—boasted a high-tech security system, the two men succeeded in entering. They moved stealthily into the family room where Jose and Kitty were dozing in front of the TV. Armed with shotguns, the killers shot off Jose's head. Alarmed, Kitty tried to escape, but she was gunned down too. When the men realized that they were out of ammunition but that Kitty was still breathing, they loaded their guns with birdshot (small pellets) and finished her off. They didn't want her to identify them to the police.

Later, when the police arrived, they found the couple dead, surrounded by pools of blood. Even though the killers tried not to leave any evidence, the identity of the two men was soon discovered: Jose and Kitty's two sons, Lyle and Eric. Only a few weeks before, the two handsome brothers had been watching a program on television called the *Billionaire Boys Club*. This show was based on a real group of young men from Beverly Hills who murdered the father of one of the group's members. Watching the movie, Lyle and Eric decided to kill their own father. He was too strict, too hard to please, and was planning to disinherit them in his will. They decided they would have to kill their mother as well since she was so emotionally dependent on their father. After long court proceedings that kept the

Meet America's Fiercest Gun Control Opponent— The NRA

The National Rifle Association (NRA) was founded in 1871 as an organization of hunters and shooters by two U.S. military officers, William C. Church and George W. Wingate. In its early days, the NRA mainly concerned itself with setting up shooting matches and creating local rifle clubs. It was only in 1934 that the NRA became politically involved in attempts to influence gun control legislation. By this time, it had become the largest and best organized association of gun owners in the United States.

Over the years, both the NRA's political influence and its numbers have grown. It has also become a powerful political lobby with a large budget and many influential members including former President Ronald Reagan and actor Charlton Heston (*The Ten Commandments* and *Planet of the Apes*). Its current membership is close to 4 million.

Lyle and Eric Menendez were sentenced in 1996 to life imprisonment without parole for the shotgun slayings of their parents.

nation riveted to the nightly news, in 1996 Lyle and Erik were finally convicted to life imprisonment without parole for the shotgun slayings of their parents.

One result of growing public concern over cases of domestic violence was a 1996 federal law that made it illegal for anyone convicted of domestic violence to keep either guns or ammunition. Other more recent laws have followed the growing number of school shootings. In the weeks that followed the Columbine High School massacre, for example, the Senate passed a flurry of gun-control legislation, which included a call for private sellers at gun shows to run background checks on buyers and a requirement that all handguns be sold with trigger locks. Currently, both houses are studying many bills, including:

- The Firearms Safety and Consumer Protection Act, a bill that would expand the powers of the secretary of the treasury to regulate the manufacture, distribution, and sale of firearms and ammunition.
- The Child Handgun Injury Prevention Act, a bill that would regulate the design, manufacture, performance of, and sale of handguns in order to prevent children from unintentionally shooting themselves.
- The Gun Show Accountability Act, a bill that would monitor the sale of firearms at gun shows.
- The Internet Gun Trafficking Act, a bill that would regulate the sale of guns over the Internet.

State and Local Gun Laws

Up until now, we have looked at the major gun control laws passed by the federal government—laws shaped by the authority of the Constitution. However, throughout the twentieth century, not only the federal government but state and even some city, or municipal, governments have passed important laws concerning gun ownership, possession, and use. After all, as we saw at the beginning of this book and as we will see later on, under the Constitution, each state was allowed to have its own militia of private citizens that could bear arms. And it fell to each state to regulate these militias and how, when, and where its citizens could use arms. This wasn't up to the federal government.

As you recall, a great fear of the Anti-Federalists was a federal government that was armed and powerful while the people were unarmed and weak. As a result (and we will explore this in the next chapter which deals with guns and the American courts), although the federal government could pass laws that affected gun use and ownership (taxing the sale of arms; enforcing the civil rights of all citizens, which indirectly meant all citizens shared the right to bear arms; regulating trade between the states, which allowed Congress to restrict gun sales from one state to another), states could, and did, pass laws that dealt directly with the right to bear arms within their borders.

Currently, there are more than 20,000 gun control laws in the United States, and the great majority of these are state and municipal laws. Just as the federal government turns to the U.S. Constitution when making federal laws, each state has its own constitution which governs

Top Three Reasons Why Murders Happen

* 31 percent are the result of an argument that became violent.

* 21 percent accompany a robbery or drug deal.

* 21 percent result from fights that are related to drinking and drugs.

the laws it can make. Since constitutions vary from state to state, so do the attitudes about guns and the type of gun laws that can be passed.

Some State Statistics

* Forty-three state constitutions give their citizens "the right to bear arms."
* Nine state constitutions permit state lawmakers to pass gun control measures.
* Seven state constitutions permit citizens to bear arms to protect their homes and families.
* Five state constitutions give citizens the right to use guns for hunting and recreational purposes.
* Two state constitutions say citizens can bear arms for the "common good."

75

• Two state constitutions prohibit nongovernment militias.

Some State Laws

Each state has its own laws concerning guns. Since the people who make laws are elected every four years, lawmakers change. This means that laws change too. If you want to be absolutely up-to-date on exactly what the gun laws are in your state or city, you should check with your local police department. Most gun laws deal with the following gun-related issues:

• Gun I.D.—a few states require gunowners to carry owner identification cards that allow police to trace a weapon to its owner.

• Carrying Guns in Plain View—in some states it is legal for a person to carry a gun out in the open.

• Carrying a Concealed Weapon—the opposite of carrying a gun in plain view is concealing it from view. Many states allow all citizens to carry concealed guns. Others give the right only to certain professionals, such as police detectives or security guards. Still others prohibit concealed weapons altogether.

• Gun Registration—some states require all guns to be registered. Large cities such as New York and Chicago, which have some of the strictest gun control laws in the country, also require registration.

Guns and Youth

American youths are more likely to die as a result of firearm use than from an accident or illness. It used to be that when teens got into an argument, it usually meant a fistfight. Unfortunately, these days, in more and more neighborhoods throughout the country, arguments often lead to or involve a shootout. For a growing number of young people, schools and neighborhoods close to home can often be dangerous places

In 1997, the CDC reported that American children were twelve times as likely to fall victim to gun-related deaths than children in the rest of the industrialized world.

According to the CDC, more than half of adolescents and young adults who kill themselves do so with a gun. Teens have turned to guns to end their lives instead of methods that might fail. While suicides have increased among younger children, suicide attempts have not, meaning that more youths are succeeding in killing themselves.

◆ Gun Purchase Permits—in some states, you have to get a license before you can even buy either a handgun or a rifle.

◆ Waiting Periods—quite a few states require for there to be a waiting period before you can buy a gun. The waiting period allows police to do a background check and to make sure that you are old enough to own a gun and that you have no criminal record. Any problem means no gun.

◆ Keeping Guns Away from Kids—many parents keep guns in the home. Many kids find them and play with them. Many guns accidentally go off, wounding or killing whoever happens to be in the way. Such accidents have led several states to require by law that parents store guns in safe places if there is a chance of kids being around or that parents put trigger locks or safety locks on their guns.

◆ Guns on School Property—you remember the story told earlier about Patrick Purdy opening fire on a school playground in Stockton, California? Well, this is only one of many such stories. And then there are the thousands of kids who confess to bringing guns to school every day. To help avoid dangerous situations, several states have passed laws prohibiting people from carrying guns on school property or onto school buses. In the meantime, more and more schools are setting up metal detectors to stop students from bringing guns into schools.

The Case of Morton Grove

Morton Grove, Illinois is a sleepy, residential town a few miles from Chicago. Guns had never been a big part of the culture there. So when a resident applied for a permit to open a gun store next to the local junior high school, citizens got upset and decided to oppose the opening of the store.

Parents didn't want their kids gazing out of the classroom window and daydreaming about guns. But since there was no federal, state, or local law they could use to refuse the permit, the only thing the city's lawmakers could do was to pass a law completely banning the sale and private use of handguns. On June 8, 1981, they did just that.

This severe attempt at gun control was the first time an American law had succeeded in actually banning (as opposed to restricting) a common firearm since the Civil War. In Morton Grove, the only people permitted to own handguns are police officers, members of the armed forces who are on duty, gun collectors, and other selected groups. Any other citizen who wants to keep or use a handgun must keep or use it at one of the town's licensed gun clubs. The successful adoption of this law led other towns in Illinois, and other parts of the United States, to pass similar laws.

• Gun Disqualification—every state disqualifies certain people from owning guns. Such people include criminals, minors, drug addicts, or people with certain mental illnesses. It is felt that guns would be extra dangerous in such people's hands.

Municipal Laws

In forty states, state gun laws cover everybody who lives in that particular state. However, in ten states, cities or municipalities are allowed to pass their own specific gun laws. This is especially common in very large cities where there is more crime. Cities like New York and Chicago have some of the toughest gun control laws in the country. New York law, for example, requires that anyone who buys a gun must get a permit. And once you have that gun, it must be registered. If you live in the boroughs of Manhattan or Brooklyn and you want a rifle, you'll have to supply four photos of yourself, be fingerprinted, and hand in two signed statements of good conduct.

Although many cities have passed laws banning guns, a couple have done just the opposite. In 1982, the small town of Kennesaw, Georgia, passed a law that obliged every head of household to keep a firearm as well as ammunition for it.

Lawyers versus Gunmakers

Meanwhile, the most recent turn in American gun control is lawyers taking on gun manufacturers and dealers on behalf of cities and states upset with rising gun-related crimes. Perhaps you've heard about the many individuals and 46 states who sued big tobacco manufacturers and won billions of dollars when it was proven that the cigarette companies knowingly sold life-threatening goods. In terms of guns, the same thing might just happen as private individuals and local communities attempt to get back some of the billions lost on gun-related violence each year.

To date, more than thirty cities (including Boston and Los Angeles) and counties have taken makers and sellers of guns to court, charging them with negligently distributing unsafe products. And in February 2000, a federal jury in Brooklyn actually found fifteen gun makers guilty of negligence in marketing and distributing their products. The municipalities say that firearms manufacturers resist low-cost trigger locks and other safety systems that could prevent so many tragic accidents at home. Furthermore, lack of control over sales and distribution allows some money-grubbing entrepreneurs to buy weapons in one state and sell them to gang members in another. And city lawyers say that the sheer size and efficiency of the profitable gun industry has become society's greatest enemy. This is because far more guns are made than are needed by law-abiding citizens. When the legal market can't absorb them, the guns go underground where they are easily bought and sold. It is said that manufacturers don't pay attention to who their dealers actually sell the guns to.

For their part, gun manufacturers and dealers say that the problem is the state and federal governments. It is the government who should be making more laws and who should be enforcing them. In response to these new charges, gun control opponents have pushed at least forty-four state governments to consider passing laws that will protect the gun industry from local and even individual lawsuits. By the middle of 2000, sixteen states, including Texas, Pennsylvania, and Virginia, had already done so.

6

The Courts and the Second Amendment

In chapter 3, we discussed the type of government the Founding Fathers created for the United States. If you recall, power was divided among three separate branches: the executive, the legislative, and the judicial. While the legislative branch is responsible for making laws, and the executive branch is responsible for carrying them out, the judicial branch must make sure that these laws are legal. Making sure that they are legal means making sure that these laws don't conflict with the law of the land contained in the Constitution.

The judicial branch of the federal government consists of the federal courts. These are courts that hear cases that come to them because somebody or some group believes that a certain new law or legal ruling is unconstitutional. After hearing a case, the court checks with the Constitution. Is this new law or ruling in accordance with the words set down by the Founding Fathers? Or does it go against these words? If there is no conflict, the federal court rules in favor of the new law or ruling. If there is a conflict, the new law or ruling is struck down as unconstitutional.

The Supreme Court

You probably already know that the United States Supreme Court is the highest court in the land. The Supreme Court's chief justice and eight associate justices are appointed for life. They are named by the president in power and are confirmed by Congress. As the highest court in the land, the Supreme Court has the power to make decisions about the Constitution and what it means. It can also declare a law of Congress unconstitutional

When the Court does decide to hear one of the many cases that have been presented to it, it judges whether or not an issue is constitutional not only by examining and interpreting the words of the Constitution, but by looking at how past courts ruled on similar issues. This is called "looking at precedent" (precedent refers to a prior decision). Although the Court might decide to overturn an earlier court's ruling, in general it uses precedent as a guide. When a decision is finally made however, not all nine judges have to be in agreement. If all are, then the decision is unanimous. Frequently, a decision has a majority opinion (that of the greater number of judges whose decision is law) and a minority or dissenting opinion (that of the one or several judges who disagree with the majority).

Because the Supreme Court is interested in the "constitutionality" of a certain issue or law, it often judges an issue or law from a different viewpoint than that of lawmakers,

America's Federal Courts: See How They Work

The United States federal court system has three levels of courts:

1. Federal District Courts. These are spread throughout the United States. These courts rule on cases in which one party charges another party with doing something considered unconstitutional. There are ninety-four of these courts.

2. Federal Courts of Appeals. If one party disagrees with the Federal District Court's ruling, they can appeal, or challenge, the ruling by taking the case to the next level: the Federal Court of Appeals. There are thirteen of these courts.

2. The Supreme Court. If, once again, a party disagrees with the judgement of the Federal Court of Appeals, they can take the case even higher: to the Supreme Court. The Supreme Court's ruling is final. After that, there is no other place to appeal. (In reality, very few cases are actually heard by the Supreme Court. Four out of nine justices must decide to hear a case. If fewer than four agree, the judgment of the lower court remains in effect.)

government officials, special interest groups, or common citizens like you and me. Throughout the history of the United States, the twenty-seven words of the Second Amendment have been interpreted in many different ways. These interpretations have depended on many factors, such as the people doing the interpreting, where they live or lived, and at what point in time they were living. A twenty-six-year-old man living in a crime-ridden neighborhood of Washington, D.C. in the 1990s will have a very different opinion about the right to bear arms than an eighty-four-year-old woman living on a farm in rural Kentucky in the 1880s or a wealthy married couple in their thirties living in a Manhattan penthouse in the 1950s. Today especially, America is becoming an increasingly diverse and varied place. It is only natural that so many different people with different realities have different opinions about what the Founding Fathers meant by those twenty-seven words, and what those words mean in today's America.

However, while parents and politicians, lawyers and law students, those who support gun control and those against it have spent much of the last two centuries (but especially the twentieth century) debating what "the right to bear and keep arms" exactly means, the Supreme Court has rarely heard cases dealing with this controversial amendment. In fact, since the Bill of Rights came into being in 1791, the Court has heard few cases that relate to the Second Amendment. And only once—in the case of The United States vs. Miller (1939)—did the Court actually rule directly on the meaning of the Second Amendment.

Supreme Court Decisions

The United States vs. Cruikshank

Following the Civil War, a Louisiana man named William Cruikshank ganged up with a few hundred other white men against newly freed black men. These racists didn't like the fact that blacks were holding a public assembly in a courthouse and that some of them had brought their firearms. So they burnt down the courthouse and murdered about 100 blacks. Among many other charges subsequently brought against them were that Cruikshank's gang attacked two black men and took their weapons away from them. At the time, under Louisiana law, the right of blacks to bear arms was restricted. When Cruikshank was charged with seizing the black men's guns, he appealed on the grounds that his crimes were not federal crimes against the United States.

As we saw in chapter 4, in 1868 the Fourteenth Amendment was added to the Constitution. It said, "No State shall make or enforce any law which shall abridge the privileges or immunities of citizens of the United States." The Fourteenth Amendment was meant to uphold the rights of all citizens, including the right to bear arms. But when the case reached the Supreme Court in 1876, the Court had to decide if the Fourteenth Amendment prevented Louisiana's state government from restricting gun ownership.

The justices of the Supreme Court claimed that they could act only if the right to bear arms (the Second Amendment) had been infringed upon by Congress. In this case, Cruikshank, accused of having committed a *federal crime*, was found not guilty. His crime did not fall under the

As the highest court in the land, the Supreme Court has the power to make decisions about the Constitution and what it means.

jurisdiction of federal law, but of state law—which in the case of Louisiana upheld racist laws against blacks.

The state law overrode both the Second Amendment and the Fourteenth Amendment. Both of these amendments protect citizens from the federal government (since the government cannot limit or take away these rights), but not from states or other private citizens

The Court's decision meant that the Second Amendment applied only to the federal government. The individual's rights were "left under the protection of the States." As such, state governments, and not the federal government, were responsible for making their own laws about ownership and the use of guns. And if they saw fit to do so, they could limit those rights.

Presser vs. Illinois

In 1885, the Supreme Court heard yet another case that dealt with the Second Amendment. A young Illinois resident named Herman Presser had organized, and led through the streets of Chicago, a small army of 400 armed German Americans. Although they carried rifles, these men were not part of the state militia or the U.S. Army. An Illinois law made it illegal for armed groups to assemble and parade in public without a permit. Accordingly, Presser was sentenced to pay a $10 fine.

Presser, however, declared this law as unconstitutional because it violated his Second Amendment right to bear arms. The Supreme Court disagreed with him and upheld the state law. According to the Court "the amendment is a limitation only upon the power of Congress and the National government, and not upon that of the States."

Although a state could not control the bearing of arms in a way that would infringe upon its militia, the state could make it illegal for citizens to bear arms for reasons that weren't military.

The Court based its ruling on the precedent of The United States vs. Cruikshank: "A State may pass laws to regulate the privileges and immunities of its own citizens, provided that in so doing it does not abridge their privileges and immunities as citizens of the United States." Its decision proved that the Court did not see the right to bear arms as an absolute right of American citizens.

Miller vs. Texas

Franklin P. Miller was tried and convicted of killing a man with a gun on the street and sentenced to death. In 1894, Miller appealed this decision on the grounds that his Second Amendment rights had been restricted by a Texas law that prohibited citizens from carrying weapons in public. Once again, the Court upheld its previous rulings. Its opinion was that Miller's rights hadn't been violated because states had the right to make their own restrictive firearms laws. This marked the third time that the Supreme Court ruled that the Second Amendment did not protect an individual's right to own or use a gun.

The United States vs. Miller

In chapter 5, we talked about the first federal law ever to restrict the keeping and bearing of arms: the National Firearms Act of 1934. When Congress passed the law, there was much opposition from those who claimed that it was unconstitutional for the federal government to infringe upon the people's rights guaranteed in the Second Amendment. The issue came up in court soon after, when Jack Miller and Frank Layton were charged with transporting a sawed-off double-barrel shotgun from one state to another without the registration and tax stamp required by the Firearms Act. A federal district court had set Miller and Layton free, arguing that the federal law violated the Second Amendment.

For the first and only time in its history, the Supreme Court was faced with the issue of a federal law that potentially limited Second Amendment rights. In a historic decision, the Court overruled the district court and upheld the federal law. The Supreme Court argued that the National Firearms Act did not violate the Second Amendment because the Second Amendment did not specifically protect the right to own and use weapons that were not useful to militias. The Court said that there was no "evidence tending to show that possession or use of a 'shotgun having a barrel of less than eighteen inches in length' at this time has some reasonable relationship to the preservation or efficiency of a well regulated militia, we cannot say that the Second Amendment guarantees the right to keep and bear such an instrument." Although the Court argued that the right to bear arms is a collective right related to militia service, it did not express an opinion concerning the Second Amendment and the individual's right to bear arms.

Lewis vs. The United States

George Calvin Lewis, Jr. had already committed a major crime when he was arrested again in Virginia in 1977 and charged with possessing an illegal gun. Under a 1968 federal law called the Omnibus Crime Control and Safe Streets Law, it was illegal for certain groups of people to own or use any type of firearm. Such groups included convicted felons, mental patients, illegal aliens, those who had been dishonorably discharged from the armed services, or those who had given up their American citizenship. Although Lewis, a convicted felon, appealed the law, saying it undermined his Second Amendment rights, the Supreme Court upheld his conviction. Basing its opinion on the precedent of *The United States vs. Miller*, the Court argued that restrictions on the sale and possession of firearms did not go against the Constitution.

The United States vs. Lopez

In 1995, the Supreme Court decided to hear a case involving Alfonzo Lopez, Jr. and a 1990 federal law called the Gun-Free School Zones Act. This law made it illegal to bring a gun within 1,000 feet of any public school. Lopez had been charged with violating this law when he entered a San Antonio, Texas high school in order to deliver a handgun to a student. Although the gun wasn't loaded, Lopez had bullets in his possession.

Lopez argued that the Gun-Free School Zones Act was unconstitutional and appealed his conviction. While one court of appeals agreed with Lopez, arguing that education is a state, and not a federal responsibility, another court of appeals decided that the Gun-Free School Zones Act was constitutional. In order to resolve the disagreement, the Supreme Court stepped in.

Although the justices were divided, the Court's final word was that the Gun-Free School Zones Act was not constitutional. The majority opinion held that Congress' powers did not extend to schools. Because public educa-

The Gun-Free School Zones Act made it illegal to bring a gun within 1,000 feet of any public school.

tion is a state matter, only states, not Congress, could pass laws dealing with it. While it didn't support bringing guns to school, the majority said that it was up to state or local governments to make the laws restricting them. The minority opinion saw the matter in a different light. Because it believed that Congress should be able to pass laws when Americans' public safety is at stake, the minority believed that the law was valid.

Printz vs. The United States

In chapter 5, we discussed how, after years of opposition, the Brady Act was finally passed into law in 1993. Of course, just because it became law, doesn't mean that the opposition gave up. The Brady Law imposed a five-day waiting period on all handgun purchases. During this waiting period, the law required state or local police to do

There are those who believe that the right to bear arms is an absolute right of each and every American citizen.

background checks on the purchasers. Jay Printz, a Montana sheriff refused to do this background check. He felt that the federal government had no right to tell a local sheriff what to do and to add to his responsibilities without paying him more.

When the Supreme Court heard this case in 1997, they agreed that the part of the Brady Law that required officers to do background checks was unconstitutional. Referring to the Tenth Amendment, which declares that all authority not given to the federal government belongs to the states, the majority sided with Printz. However, even though officers were no longer required to do background checks, the part of the Brady Act that required a five-day waiting period still remained in effect. The minority, who had supported the Brady Act in its entirety, believed that Congress did in fact have authority to respond to escalating gun violence. They quoted a Department of Justice report claiming that "between 1994 and 1996, approximately 6,600 firearms sales each month to potentially dangerous persons were prevented by Brady Act checks; over 70 percent of the rejected purchasers were convicted or indicted felons."

Ultimately, the Supreme Court has been very cautious about interpreting the Second Amendment. Because of this they have heard very few cases that directly concern the exact meaning of the controversial right to bear arms. What the Court has done is to declare that the Second Amendment does not give an individual citizen the absolute right to bear arms. State, local, and federal governments can all pass laws that restrict the individual possession or use of firearms. And these laws are not considered unconstitutional. Of course, there are many laws that are never judged by the Supreme Court. As was mentioned before, most of the 20,000 gun control laws in existence are state and local laws, which vary from place to place. It is logical therefore that their legality is often questioned, and ruled upon, in state courts.

State Court Decisions

As we saw in the previous chapter, forty-three out of fifty American states have constitutions that protect the right to bear arms. Just as the Supreme Court bases its rulings on the words of the United States Constitution, the state courts base theirs on the text of their own constitutions, most of which have clauses similar to the Second Amendment.

Early on, state courts seemed hesitant about placing limits on their citizens' right to bear arms. Kentucky was the first state to take the plunge. The year was 1813 and the state's law prohibiting its citizens from carrying concealed weapons was the first of its kind in America. Kentucky was also the first state to make a court decision on the right to bear arms. In 1822, in the case of *Bliss vs. Commonwealth*, the court heard the appeal of a man who had been convicted of walking around town with a sword concealed in his cane. The charges were dropped when the court decided that the right to bear arms meant bearing all arms, not just those carried in plain view. The court's decision was based on the Kentucky Constitution that stated that "the right of citizens to bear arms in defense of themselves and the State must be preserved . . . "

A similar case occurred some years later in Georgia. In 1837, the state had passed a law banning the sale of most pistols. In 1846, the Georgia Supreme Court overturned this law. It found the law unconstitutional and based its argument on the second clause of the Second Amendment which it interpreted as "the right of the whole people, old and young, men, women and boys, and not militia only, to keep and bear arms of every description, and not such merely as are used by the militia, shall not be infringed, curtailed, or broken in upon, in the smallest degree."

These early decisions were particular because they declared that an individual citizen's right to bear arms was absolute. As the nineteenth century wore on, society would change and so would gun culture. Reflecting these changes would be the attitude of the courts, which began to uphold restrictions on ownership and possession of arms.

As early as the 1840s, state courts began to support weapon control laws. In 1840, in Aymette vs. the State, the Supreme Court of Tennessee based its support of a state gun control law on the state constitution, which declared "that the citizens of this State have a right to keep and to bear arms for their common defense; but the Legislature shall have power, by law, to regulate the wearing of arms with a view to prevent crime." Other state courts made many other similar decisions based on similar clauses in their constitutions. The result was that while courts supported citizens' keeping arms, they felt that the states had the right to step in and regulate their use in order to ensure public peace and safety.

This view—that the right to keep and bear arms can be restricted, or even prohibited, by the government—has continued to dominate thousands of state and local court decisions throughout the twentieth century as well. At the same time however, some courts have also ruled that the right to keep and bear arms means that individual citizens do have a right to keep weapons such as handguns and revolvers for purposes of self-defense. The supreme courts of Montana, Colorado, and Oregon all based such decisions on their own state constitutions.

In a 1980 case, for example, the Supreme Court of Oregon explained its ruling in the following manner: "We are not unmindful that there is current controversy over the wisdom of the right to bear arms, and that the original motivations for such a provision might not seem compelling if debated as a new issue. Our task, however . . . is to respect the principles given the status of constitutional guarantees and limitations by the drafters; it is not to abandon these principles when this fits the needs of the moment."

The court must have realized that its decision to let individuals bear arms for self-defense would be opposed by supporters of gun control. However, it based its decision on its state's constitution which said: "the people shall have the right to bear arms for the defense of themselves, and the State."

7 American Citizens and the Second Amendment

In the two preceding chapters, we saw how American judges, lawmakers, and politicians have interpreted and reacted to the Second Amendment. We looked at gun laws that were passed and gun laws that were overturned. We looked at how the right to bear arms was restricted or expanded at different moments in history and in different parts of this country. But perhaps most important is how private citizens like you, your friends, parents, and neighbors view guns in our society.

The right to bear arms is a very serious and complicated issue. After all, guns are quite literally a matter of life and death. And the United States of America has a very serious gun problem, with gun-related murders, accidents, suicides, and violence that far outnumber those of other industrialized nations. At the same time, the right to bear arms is part of American culture and history. It is a fundamental right that guarantees citizens the right to protect themselves, their homes, and their loved ones.

99

What then is the solution? Is it placing even more restrictions on guns? Is it banning them altogether? Is it requiring young people to learn about gun safety and how to shoot accurately? These questions are difficult to answer. However, as America steps into the twenty-first century, more and more people are trying. Although many voices are speaking out and being heard, almost all can be divided into one of two camps.

There are those who believe that the right to bear arms is an absolute right of each and every American citizen. These people are known as gun control opponents. They see every bill or law that places restrictions on gun ownership or use as an infringement of their fundamental American rights guaranteed under the Second Amendment.

Then there are those who believe that America has changed significantly since the Founding Fathers drafted the Constitution. They believe that the common safety and security of everybody is more important than the non-essential right of an individual. They believe that gun-related violence in this country is out of hand. And the only way to control it is to create laws that limit or even ban ownership and use of guns.

As you will discover, both those who support and those who oppose gun control have interesting, logical, and valid arguments. They use these arguments to make Americans aware of the role of guns in society. They also use them to lobby lawmakers of both state and federal governments. Lobbying is an organized attempt to influence lawmakers to vote for or against a specific law. As you discover both opponents' and supporters' points of view, think hard about where you and the people you know stand on gun control.

Americans Most Likely to Own Guns Are:

- Male
- White
- Older
- Southern
- Earn more than $20,000 a year
- Live in rural areas

Opponents of Gun Control

Patty was on the verge of falling asleep when she thought she heard her teenage daughter let out a muffled scream. Patty reached towards her dresser, and unlocked the top drawer. She pulled out her handgun and silently crept out of her room and down the stairs. The living room lights were on and Patty saw her daughter struggling with a stranger in a ski mask. "Let her go and put your hands up—or I'll shoot!" yelled Patty, loudly but firmly. The stranger let go of her daughter and put his hands up, dropping a knife to the floor. Shaking, Patty kept her gun aimed at the man, while she called the police. She was terrified to think what would have happened to her daughter if she hadn't had a gun at that moment.

Many people feel that owning a gun is a fundamental American right. Some in particular want to be ready and able to protect themselves from armed and dangerous criminals.

People like Patty are really glad for a Second Amendment that allows them to protect themselves and their loved ones. They feel that owning a gun is a fundamental right. They also feel that with so many armed and dangerous criminals running around, they have no choice but to have a gun and to know how to use it. It's not as if Patty is gun crazy or is a violent person. But she feels that if she had just stayed in her bedroom, dialed 911, and waited for the police to show up, things could have ended very differently for both her daughter and herself.

Bill Potter was at his favorite burger place. He was slurping down the last of his cola, when suddenly, a young guy in army fatigues charged out of the bathroom, and pointed a semiautomatic at the restaurant manager's head. The guy hollered for the terrified young employee to empty the register or he'd "blow a hole" in his head.

The restaurant erupted in panic as customers screamed and ducked down under their tables. From where Bill was beneath his table, he could see the young guy's trigger hand trembling as the manager fumbled with the cash register. "You're taking too long!" screamed the gunman. He pulled the trigger and the employee fell to the floor. Everybody in the restaurant starting screaming in fear, which only upset the gunman more. He randomly aimed his semiautomatic and started firing off bullets around the restaurant. Then he jerked open the cash register, grabbed $246, and ran off.

Three people died that day. Seven more were seriously wounded. When the police arrived soon after, Bill confessed that if only he had been carrying his gun, he could have saved these people's lives. Bill was an excellent gunman. From where he was crouched, he could have taken that young punk out without endangering anybody. Bill thought it was stupid that the year before, the state in which he lived had passed a law making it illegal to carry concealed weapons in public. If this hold-up had occurred over a year ago, Bill would have been armed and prepared. He could have stopped this tragedy from happening.

Like Patty, Bill is against laws that seek to restrict gun control. He and many others think that the Constitution gave all Americans the right to bear arms. They feel it is unjust and unconstitutional to limit this right. And they point to episodes like Bill's burger joint hold-up as reasons why private citizens should be armed. They fear that eventually, law-abiding citizens will be defenseless and unarmed, unable to protect themselves against the growing number of criminals who buy and carry guns illegally.

Major Arguments Against Gun Control

• The Second Amendment of the U.S. Constitution—the "law of the land"—gives each American citizen "the right to keep and bear arms."

• The majority of state constitutions give individual citizens the right to bear arms.

• Police can't be everywhere at once. By the time they arrive at the scene of a crime, the damage has already been done.

Shopping for Guns

By 1996, Sears, J.C. Penney, and Target had all stopped selling guns. Not only were they not making any money, but they also worried about being held responsible if guns were misused. They also thought that having guns on their shelves undermined the family image they were trying to project. This is why Wal-Mart doesn't keep handguns in their stores—but you can order them by catalog.

• Protecting oneself and one's family and property is the right and the duty of every American citizen.

• Criminals are afraid of guns. Statistics show that they are less likely to attack, assault, rape, rob, or break into the house of somebody if they suspect or know that person owns a gun.

• Gun control affects the 20 million Americans who like to hunt for recreation. Hunters claim that registration and licensing fees that gun control laws impose on them make this traditional American sport unaffordable for many people.

• Gun control has done nothing to reduce crime. Opponents point to many situations in which states or cities passed laws restricting the purchase or possession of certain types of firearms only to find that gun-related crimes increased. They feel the solution is not restricting guns (which only hurts law-abiding citizens—criminals can always buy a gun illegally off the street), but toughening crime laws and increasing prison terms for convicted criminals.

A Few Citizens Speak Out For Guns

"Laws that forbid the carrying of arms . . . disarm only those who are neither inclined nor determined to commit crimes. Such laws make things worse for the assaulted and better for the assailants; they serve rather to encourage than to prevent homicides, for an unarmed man may be attacked with greater confidence than an armed man."

—*Thomas Jefferson, former U.S. president*

"The right of citizens to bear arms is just one more guarantee against arbitrary government, one more safeguard against the tyranny which now appears remote in America, but which historically has proved to be always possible."

—*Hubert Humphrey, former U.S. vice president*

"The right to own and use firearms is the preeminent individual right. Without the ability to physically defend . . . our Constitution . . . the remainder of the Bill of Rights become privileges granted by the government and subject to restrictions at the whim of the government."

—*J. Warren Cassidy, executive vice president, NRA*

Why Do Adults Keep Guns at Home?

♦ 45 percent for hunting or recreation
♦ 37 percent for protection from criminals
♦ 5 percent are collectors
♦ 2 percent need a gun as a job requirement
♦ 10 percent say some other reason
♦ 1 percent are not sure

Gun Organizations

There are quite a few organizations that oppose gun control and support the right of private citizens to own and use guns. Some of the best known include the Second Amendment Foundation and the Citizens Committee for the Right to Keep and Bear Arms. Of course, the biggest, most organized, and most influential of these organizations is the National Rifle Association.

The NRA fiercely defends individuals' rights to bear arms and they organize a great many public awareness campaigns to convince the public that the violence in America is not caused by guns, but by people. Well-organized and with a large budget, the organization fiercely fights any attempt at creating new gun control laws. They see each new law as a further restriction of a fundamental American right. The NRA's position is summed up in their famous slogan: "Guns don't kill, people do."

The NRA says the problem is not guns themselves but people who don't know how to use them. To try and fix this, the NRA has developed gun safety and awareness programs in communities throughout the U.S. And in 1990, it launched a gun safety campaign aimed specifically at kids. "Learn Gun Safety with Eddie Eagle" features a cartoon eagle named Eddie who lets kids know that guns aren't toys. Eddie gives safety tips and teaches kids what to do if they come across a gun (get away from it and then tell an adult).

Supporters of Gun Control

One Friday night, Maya drove her fifteen-year-old daughter, Amalia, to a friend's party. It was the last time she ever saw her. At 11:30, Amalia called from the party to tell her mom she needn't bother coming to pick her up. She would get a ride home with her friend Jason.

Amalia and Jason left the party a little before midnight. On the way home they stopped at a gas station. While Jason filled up the tank, Amalia went inside the twenty-four-hour convenience store to buy some sugarless gum. She was just handing over some change when a hooded thug came in with a gun and started shooting everybody in sight, including Amalia. When the ambulance arrived at 12:30, Amalia was already dead.

Stories like Amalia's are all too common in the United States these days. In 1995, 20,043 people were murdered in

The Case of Our Capital

Washington, D.C. has one of the worst violent crime rates of any city in the United States. In our nation's capital, 75 out of every 100,000 residents are murdered. The national average is 9.5 out of every 100,000.

In 1976, a law was passed banning handguns. However, almost twenty years later, a 1994 report showed that 304 of the city's 309 murders that year had been committed with a handgun. In fact, since handguns were banned, Washington's murder rate has more than tripled. Gun control opponents claim that restrictions on private ownership of guns is responsible for this high crime rate. "What has the gun control law done to keep criminals from getting guns? Absolutely nothing . . . [Citizens] ought to have the opportunity to have a handgun."

California Dreaming (More Like a Nightmare)

Although California has a ban on assault weapons and a fifteen-day waiting period on handgun sales, the state's murder rate is 38 percent higher than the rest of the country's.

Nothing Could Be Finer Than to Be in Carolina?

When South Carolina passed a law limiting handgun sales to one per month per person, there was a 100 percent increase in violent crime.

Meanwhile, in Kennesaw…

At the end of chapter 5, we took a look at Kennesaw, a town in Georgia that passed a law requiring all heads of households to keep a gun at home. Since the law came into effect in 1982, there has been a 16 percent decrease in crime—and this in spite of the fact that the population has doubled.

the U.S. This works out to one murder every twenty-four minutes. In terms of young people, the stats are really alarming. The scary truth is that an average of thirteen teens are killed by guns each day in this country. It is hardly surprising that gunfire is currently the second leading cause of death in American young people between the ages of ten and nineteen.

Congressional hearings have featured testimony by many witnesses who tell stories about how having a gun saved their lives and/or the lives of others. Most of these stories are very convincing. However, these stories are often selected to reinforce a point of view. Equally convincing stories can be told about people who are killed or seriously injured when they pull out their guns and try to defend themselves.

There are untold stories about people who bought guns to protect themselves and their homes and wound up killing themselves or others because they didn't know how to handle a gun. And although the NRA teaches courses in gun safety, it opposes any law that would make such training obligatory before obtaining a license to buy a gun. Statistics show that 45 percent of all people who try to defend themselves with guns become gun victims instead. Worse, hardly a week goes by without a news story about a child who was shot, hurt, or killed by a gun kept in the home in the honest belief that it was there for protection:

In Mississippi, a two-year-old boy toddled into the living room to check out the Christmas tree lights. In his excitement, he jumped up and down. His movement set off a burglar alarm. Hearing the alarm, his mother panicked. Snatching her semi-automatic, she ran to the living room and fired at the first thing she saw moving—her son.

The Multiple Meanings of "Militia"

"A well regulated Militia, being necessary to the security of a free State, the right of the people to keep and bear Arms, shall not be infringed."

How can twenty-seven words create so much controversy? The trouble is that some words have multiple meanings. Perhaps no word has created more confusion than "militia."

Back in the 1700s, when the Bill of Rights was drawn up, "militia" referred to the male population capable of bearing arms. This meant that nearly everyone was in the militia. Thus, say gun control opponents, everyone has the right to keep and bear arms. Times change, however. Today, "militia" often refers to an army made up of trained citizens who are not professional soldiers. According to gun control advocates, this means that only a select group of trained people, and not the entire United States population, has the right to keep and bear arms.

The actual role of militias has changed as well. In the 1700s, the United States had no army. Each state had a separate militia made up of healthy males. They owned arms in order to defend themselves and their country. Today, however, there are the U.S. armed forces and a national guard for each state. These men and women are trained to use arms to protect citizens and defend their country. Private citizens no longer need to be soldiers, so they no longer need to bear arms to protect their country.

In California, an eleven-year-old boy discovered a pistol under his parents' bed. He showed it to his two-year-old stepsister and warned, "Don't ever play with this." Unfortunately, as he did so the pistol went off, killing the little girl.

In Louisiana, a young girl decided to surprise her dad. She hid in the coat closet and when her dad came home from work late one night, she jumped out and yelled, "Boo!" Startled, her dad pulled out the concealed gun he was carrying and shot her dead.

In New York, a woman discovered a handgun in the garbage and put it in her desk drawer. Her seven-year-old son found it. Not knowing that it was real, he and his little brother started playing with it. The boy ended up shooting his five-year-old brother in the head.

In Georgia, a three-year-old boy caught sight of something sticking out from under his mother's mattress. He reached in to pull the object out. The part of the object he grabbed onto was the gun's trigger. He squeezed it and shot himself in the face.

People who support gun control feel that the gun situation has gotten out of control in the United States. The number of shootings in schools, homes, and offices across the country has mobilized many people who feel something needs to be done. Their solution is more gun control. Gun control can mean many things. It can mean requiring people who buy guns to register them so that the guns can be traced.

A Few Citizens Speak Out Against Guns

"Violence has accompanied virtually every stage and aspect of our national existence [and] it has been a determinant of both the form and substance of American life. We have resorted so often to violence that we have long since become a trigger-happy people."

—Richard Maxwell Brown, author of *Historical Patterns of Violence: Violence in America*.

"Our complex society requires a rethinking of the proper role of firearms in modern America. Our forefathers used firearms as an integral part of their struggle for survival. But today firearms are not appropriate for daily life in the United States."

—Edward Kennedy, Massachusetts Senator

"How much more horrifying can the evidence get, before it becomes clear to all that guns . . . are too easily obtained, kept and used in this country, by almost anyone?"

—Tom Wicker, *New York Times* journalist

Many people do not believe that the Second Amendment gives
individual citizens absolute rights to keep and bear arms.

It can mean having a waiting period which allows police to do a background check on the purchaser. It can mean having a license to own and carry a gun. It can mean prohibiting or limiting the sale, ownership, or possession of certain types of firearms in certain places, or prohibiting certain people from owning guns. It can mean obliging gun owners to store their arms safely. It can mean putting safety locks on guns and triggers for which only owners have the key or combination.

Gun control supporters feel that the federal government is the only one with the power to control the arms industries and people's access to guns. Few believe that guns should be banned completely. But they do feel that too many guns are ending up too easily in the wrong hands.

Most gun control advocates respect the Second Amendment. However, they tend to have a different interpretation of this controversial amendment. Many don't believe that it gives individual citizens absolute rights to keep and bear arms. Instead they see the amendment as a collective right of a state's "militia" to bear arms in order to defend themselves. A staunch supporter of this viewpoint is former Supreme Court Chief Justice Warren Burger who once argued: "Is there any question that a citizen has the right to own and keep an automobile? Yet we accept the state's power to regulate its purchase and to license the vehicle and its driver. Should guns be any different?"

Arguments For Gun Control

♦ The Second Amendment does not give individual citizens the absolute right to keep and bear arms.

115

◆ Throughout American history, state courts, federal courts, and the Supreme Court have ruled that both federal and state governments have the right to limit the private ownership and use of guns.

◆ The United States is not the same place it was more than two centuries ago when guns were necessary for survival (hunting food, protection from hostile Indians, self-protection in the absence of police).

◆ Gun-related violence and deaths are a major social problem that just keeps getting worse. In 1994, close to 40,000 Americans died from gunshot wounds.

◆ Other industrialized nations with strict gun control laws have many fewer murders, suicides, and gun-related deaths and injuries. In 1992, for example, Japan had sixty handgun murders. The U.S. had 13,000. Japan has half the population of the U.S. It also has strict gun laws that almost completely prohibit private citizens from owning handguns.

◆ Around 50 percent of American households contain at least one gun. Fifty-four percent of American high school-aged teens live in a house with at least one gun in it. Homes with guns are 4.8 times more likely to be the scene of a suicide and 2.7 times more likely to be the scene of a murder than similar homes without guns.

◆ School shootings are increasing in number. So are young victims of gunshot wounds. Nearly 135,000 kids take guns to school every day. A

Is It Ever Okay to Shoot Someone?

Bernhard Goetz, a thirty-six-year-old engineer from New York, was sitting on the subway, minding his own business, when four young African American men approached him and asked him for $5. Goetz believed he was being threatened. He pulled out a revolver and fired at the youths. To many people, he was, and is, a hero.

After a hurricane hit southern Florida, residents put up signs on the wreckage of their homes and businesses that read "YOU LOOT, WE SHOOT!" Many applauded.

During the Los Angeles riots following the first trial of the police officers accused in the Rodney King beating, some owners of small businesses sat on their roofs armed with rifles, ready to fire at looters. And hardly a week goes by in New York City when some shopkeeper is not proclaimed a hero for shooting at a robber.

+ 10 percent of teens agree with the statement, "It is okay to shoot a person if that is what it takes to get something you want."

+ 10 percent of teens agree with the statement, "It is okay to shoot some guy who does not belong in your neighborhood."

+ 28 percent of teens agree with the statement, "It is okay to shoot someone who insulted you."

What do you think?

117

Marchers at the Million Mom March, the nation's largest-ever gun control rally, demanded tougher gun control.

national survey found that one in twenty high school students had carried a gun to school in the past month.

◆ The medical costs of treating gunshot wounds are enormous. The average cost of treating a child who has been shot is $15,000. Every year, $4 billion is spent treating gun-related injuries in the United States.

◆ Gun control works, if enforced. The first year after the 1993 passage of the Brady Act, which placed a five-day waiting period on handgun purchases, 4,365 convicted criminals were prevented from buying guns.

The State of the Gun Control Debate Today

On May 14, 2000, hundreds of thousands of Americans thronged Washington, D.C.'s National Mall demanding tougher gun control. Dubbed the Million Mom March—it was held on Mother's Day and was largely made-up of moms from all over America—the march was the largest-ever gun control rally in U.S. history. Marching mothers, many whose children had been wounded or killed by firearms, carried banners with slogans such as "Guns Don't Die, People Do." Among them were famous moms such as Susan Sarandon, Rosie O'Donnell, and Hillary Rodham Clinton. There were also moms like Veronica McQueen. Her six-year-old daughter, Kayla, had been shot and killed earlier that year. The murder had taken place in her first grade classroom in Flint, Michigan. Kayla's assassin was a six-year-old classmate with a gun.

Also marching in Washington that day were some moms who called themselves the Second Amendment Sisters. Fewer in number, they were nonetheless fierce supporters of their right to bear arms.

No matter which group one was marching with, it was obvious that the issue of gun control in America was being more fiercely debated than ever before. And for the first time, it looked as if it was going to be one of the most important, if not the most important, issues of the presidential campaign of 2000. Although few politicians attended the popular rally, both presidential candidates were forced to take stands and offer solutions. Vice President Al Gore, the Democratic candidate, had already talked about a plan for registration and a requirement that guns be "childproofed" with a special safety lock. Meanwhile, his Republican rival, Texas Governor George W. Bush, stuck to more modest plans such as free distribution of trigger locks and tougher enforcement of laws already in existence.

In the meantime however, NRA membership is at an all-time high. One week after the moms marched on Washington, an NRA rally in Charlotte, North Carolina brought thousands of gun control opponents into the streets. Blaming Hollywood and other media for America's violence, many wore t-shirts that read: "Guns Save Lives." By the time Bush was voted into the White House, the country's largest anti-gun control organizations will boast four million members. Who will end up having the greatest influence on presidents and politicians, judges and lawyers, parents and kids, people like me and you all over the country? What changes—if any—will be made in the interpretation of the Second Amendment; in the laws that allow and restrict the right to bear arms; in the behavior and attitudes of everyday Americans faced with gun-related violence?

8 Gun Culture in America Today

We are now at the beginning of a new millennium and a new century, and the role of guns in our society has never been as hotly debated as it is today. At the same time, guns seem to be everywhere. They star in popular movies and are featured on prime-time TV shows. They are all over the news as one five-year-old in kindergarten pulls the trigger on another and rival gangs in our nation's capital shoot up the zoo, and some innocent bystanders, on African American Family Day.

April 20, 2000 marked the one-year anniversary of the massacre at Columbine High School that left 15 people dead. An independent survey found that 66 percent of Americans think gun control is more important than the rights of gun owners (29 percent think the opposite). Yet many of these same Americans, like members of the NRA and other gun control opponents, doubt that tighter restrictions will solve the problem of gun-related violence in this country. Many believe community programs for young people and tougher prison terms would be much more effective than tougher gun laws. Only 6 percent of those surveyed thought stricter gun laws could have prevented a tragedy like Columbine.

What About the Rest of the World?

Much of the rest of the world thinks that America is a violent place. In almost no other part of the world are private citizens as free to own and use guns as in the United States. The mass production of guns and their constant presence on television, in films, and in the press has made them a big part of American life. So has the Second Amendment.

We are the only developed nation in which guns are such a big part of the culture. It is believed that Americans own over 220 million firearms. That is close to

NATION	ANY GUN	HANDGUN	TOTAL MURDERS	MURDERS BY GUN
Australia	19.6	2.0	19.5	6.6
Canada	29.1	6.0	18.5	8.7
England	4.7	0.1	6.7	0.8
France	22.6	6.0	12.5	5.5
Holland	1.9	0.2	11.8	2.7
Norway	38.7	4.0	12.1	3.6
Spain	13.1	2.5	13.7	3.8
U.S.	48.0	29.0	75.9	44.6

one gun for every man, woman, and child in the country. These are very high numbers for a nation with secure borders, a nuclear defense system, and armed police. A big difference between the United States and the other countries mentioned in the chart on page 123 is that all the other countries have very strict gun control laws. Citizens who are allowed to own guns must go through waiting periods, register their arms, and have licenses to use them. Gun control advocates point to these countries and their tight gun laws as model examples of what could happen in the U.S. if more restrictions were placed on guns. Yet aside from the fact that it is much more difficult to simply get a gun in these countries, there is also an important cultural factor involved. Many citizens of these other countries quite simply don't want or don't feel they need a gun. Guns are not—and never have been—part of their culture.

An interesting exception to the examples above is the case of Switzerland. In this tiny European country, a larger percentage of private citizens own guns than in the U.S. This is because instead of relying on a permanent army, Switzerland depends on a militia of armed citizens for defense. As a result, almost every adult male is legally obliged to own a gun. The Swiss government actually supplies enlisted men with automatic assault weapons and pistols. At the same time, Switzerland has one of the lowest gun-related murder rates of any industrialized nation. Gun control opponents say this proves that the problem in America isn't guns themselves, it's the people who use, or misuse, them.

This raises some complicated questions. Why then is there so much violence in America today? Is it due to the presence of so many guns? Or is it people's attitudes in relation to guns? Are there just too many violent individuals in the United States? Or is our society as a whole violent? Maybe a combination of these factors is to blame. Or perhaps the blame lies somewhere else altogether. What do you think?

Timeline: A History of Guns in America

1770—Tension between colonists and British troops leads to Boston Massacre.

1776—Declaration of Independence is proclaimed in protest of British colonial rule.

1776—Virginia is the first state to create its own declaration of rights, which includes a provision for an armed militia.

1787—U.S. Constitution is written in Philadelphia.

1789—James Madison proposes amendments to the Constitution.

1791—Adoption of the Bill of Rights with its ten Amendments.

1813—Kentucky is the first state to pass a law prohibiting citizens from carrying concealed weapons.

1822—In Bliss vs. Commonwealth, Kentucky overturns the 1813 gun control law.

1835—When the federal government forces Native Americans to move west to reservations, it provides them with guns.

1849—Discovery of gold in California brings settlers charging west. Congress gives them guns for protection.

1862—Black Americans are accepted into Union militias during the Civil War.

1865—With the end of the Civil War, Southern states adopt "black codes" that restrict blacks from owning and using guns.

1866—Congress passes the Civil Rights Act, which protects rights of all American citizens, regardless of color and guarantees these rights by adding the Fourteenth Amendment to the Constitution.

1871—National Rifle Association is founded as an organization for hunters and sportsmen.

1876—*The United States vs. Cruikshank.* The U.S. Supreme Court decides that the Second Amendment applies only to the federal government, not to state governments.

1886—*Presser vs. Illinois.* The U.S. Supreme Court rules that states can restrict the right to bear arms as long as a strong state militia is maintained.

1894—*Miller vs. Texas.* The U.S. Supreme Court upholds a state law which prohibits the carrying of deadly weapons.

1911—The state of New York passes the Sullivan Law which limits the sale, possession, and use of deadly weapons.

1919—Congress passes the War Revenues Act, the first tax on sales of firearms.

1927—The Miller Bill, limiting mail-order sales of concealable guns, becomes a federal law.

1934—To cut down on "gangster weapons," Congress passes the National Firearms Act, the first federal law to restrict the keeping and bearing of firearms.

1938—The Federal Firearms Act gives the federal government more control over gun sales.

1939—*United States vs. Miller.* The U.S. Supreme Court upholds the National Firearms Act of 1934.

1963—President John F. Kennedy is assassinated in Dallas, Texas

1965—Muslim minister and black rights leader Malcolm X is assassinated in New York City.

1968—Civil rights leader Dr. Martin Luther King, Jr. is assassinated in Memphis, Tennessee, in April. Presidential candidate Robert F. Kennedy is assassinated in Los Angeles, in June. The Gun Control Act is passed by Congress in an attempt to control gun-related violence.

1977—*Lewis vs. the United States.* The U.S. Supreme Court decides that certain groups of people can be banned from owning or using firearms.

1979—Last restrictions on Native American gun ownership are lifted.

1981—President Ronald Reagan escapes an assassination attempt that critically injures his press secretary James Brady. The Handgun Crime Control Act, which includes a seven-day waiting period for the purchase of a handgun, is introduced to Congress, but fails to pass. Morton Grove, a town in Illinois, completely bans the sale or possession of handguns.

1986—Congress passes the Firearms Owners Protection Act which repeals parts of the 1968 Gun Control Act by allowing sale and transportation of firearms between states. Congress bans manufacture and sale of machine guns to individuals and bans plastic guns.

1989—Congress bans import of forty-three types of assault weapons as a result of a schoolyard shooting spree in California that leaves five children dead.

1993—The Brady Bill finally becomes federal law.

1996—The U.S. Supreme Court declares part of the 1993 Brady Act, in which state officers are required to do background checks on gun purchasers, unconstitutional.

1999—Columbine High School Massacre: Two teens armed with shotguns kill thirteen people before killing themselves at their high school in Littleton, Colorado.

2000—A federal jury in Brooklyn finds fifteen gun makers guilty of negligence in marketing and distributing their products. The Million Mom March in Washington is the largest-ever gun control rally. The NRA's membership approaches an all-time high of 4 million.

Preamble to the Constitution

We the People of the United States, in order to form a more perfect Union, establish Justice, insure domestic Tranquility, provide for the common defence, promote the general Welfare, and secure the Blessings of Liberty to ourselves and our Posterity, do ordain and establish this Constitution for the United States of America.

On September 25, 1789, Congress transmitted to the state legislatures twelve proposed amendments, two of which, having to do with congressional representation and congressional pay, were not adopted. The remaining ten amendments became the Bill of Rights.

The Bill of Rights

Amendment I

Congress shall make no law respecting an establishment of religion, or prohibiting the free exercise thereof; or abridging the freedom of speech, or of the press; or the right of the people peaceably to assemble, and to petition the Government for a redress of grievances.

Amendment II

A well regulated Militia, being necessary to the security of a free State, the right of the people to keep and bear Arms, shall not be infringed.

Amendment III

No Soldier shall, in time of peace be quartered in any house, without the consent of the Owner, nor in time of war, but in a manner to be prescribed by law.

Amendment IV

The right of the people to be secure in their persons, houses, papers, and effects, against unreasonable searches and seizures, shall not be violated, and no Warrants shall issue, but upon probable cause, supported by Oath or affirmation, and particularly describing the place to be searched, and the persons or things to be seized.

Amendment V

No person shall be held to answer for a capital, or otherwise infamous crime, unless on a presentment or indictment of a Grand Jury, except in cases arising in the land or naval forces, or in the Militia, when in actual service in time of War or public danger; nor shall any person be subject for the same offence to be twice put in jeopardy of life or limb; nor shall be compelled in any criminal case to be a witness against himself, nor be deprived of life, liberty, or property, without due process of law; nor shall private property be taken for public use, without just compensation.

Amendment VI

In all criminal prosecutions, the accused shall enjoy the right to a speedy and public trial, by an impartial jury of the State and district wherein the crime shall have been committed, which district shall have been previously ascertained by law, and to be informed of the nature and cause of the accusation; to be confronted with the witnesses against him; to have compulsory process for obtaining witnesses in his favor, and to have the Assistance of Counsel for his defence.

Amendment VII

In Suits at common law, where the value in controversy shall exceed twenty dollars, the right of trial by jury shall be preserved, and no fact tried by a jury, shall be otherwise re-examined in any Court of the United States, than according to the rules of the common law.

Amendment VIII

Excessive bail shall not be required, nor excessive fines imposed, nor cruel and unusual punishments inflicted.

Amendment IX

The enumeration in the Constitution, of certain rights, shall not be construed to deny or disparage others retained by the people.

Amendment X

The powers not delegated to the United States by the Constitution, nor prohibited by it to the States, are reserved to the States respectively, or to the people.

Glossary

amendment
Addition to the U.S. Constitution.

appeal
When the ruling of a lower court is challenged and the case is then heard by a higher court.

automatic rifle
Rifle that fires one bullet after another when the trigger is pulled and held. Also referred to as a machine gun.

ban
To prohibit.

bayonet
Dagger-like piece of steel placed on the muzzle of a gun which allowed a soldier to finish off one's enemy by stabbing.

constitutional
Something that is in accordance with the U.S. Constitution.

felony
Serious crime, such as murder, rape, or robbery.

gun control
Laws that restrict how or whether a person may buy, sell, or own a gun.

handgun
Small handheld firearm such as a pistol or revolver.

militia
Army of private citizens that is called upon in times of emergency.

musket
Heavy five-to-seven foot firearm, worn slung over the shoulder, that was an ancestor of the rifle.

ratification
Approval of a measure, law, or amendment.

rifle
Shoulder gun in which spiral grooves cut inside the barrel put a spin on shot bullets, making them more accurate.

Saturday night special
Cheap, poorly made handgun.

waiting period
Short period of time between applying to buy a gun and actually getting one, during which police can check the buyer's background.

For More Information

Bureau of Alcohol, Tobacco and Firearms
650 Massachusetts Avenue, NW
Washington, DC 20226
(202) 927-7777
Web site: http://www.atf.treas.gov

Center to Prevent Handgun Violence
1225 Eye Street NW, Suite 1100
Washington, DC 20005
(202) 898-0792
Web site: http://www.handguncontrol.org

Citizens' Committee for the Right to Keep and Bear Arms
12500 NE Tenth Place
Bellevue, WA 98005
(800) 426-4302
Web site: http://www.ccrkba.org

Coalition to Stop Gun Violence
1000 16th Street NW, Suite 603
Washington, DC 20036-5705
(202) 530-0340
Web site: http://www.gunfree.org

Federal Bureau of Investigation
935 Pennsylvania Avenue NW
Washington, DC 20535-0001
(202) 324-3000
Web site: http://www.fbi.gov

Gun Owners of America
8001 Forbes Plaza, Suite 102
Springfield, VA 22151
(703) 321-8585
Web site: http://www.gunowners.org

The Lawyer's Second Amendment Society
1077 W. Morton Avenue, Suite C
Porterville, CA 93257-1989
Web site: http://www.thelsas.org

National Institute of Justice
810 Seventh Street NW
Washington, DC 20531
Tel: (202) 307-2942
http://www.ojp.usdoj.gov/nij

National Rifle Association
11250 Waples Mill Road, Suite 1
Fairfax, VA 22030
(703) 267-1000
Web site: http://www.nra.org

Supreme Court of the United States
1 First Street NE
Washington, DC 20543
(202) 479-3211
Web site: http://www.supremecourtus.gov

Violence Policy Center
1140 19th Street NW, Suite 600
Washington, DC 20036
(202) 822-8200
Web site: http://www.vpc.org

Web Sites

The Crime Library
http://www.crimelibrary.com

Educate the U.S.A.
http://www.unitedstates-on-line.com

Find Law Guide
http://www.findlaw.com

Supreme Court of the United States
http://www.supremecourtus.gov

Thomas Legislative Information on the Internet from the Library of Congress
http://lcweb2.loc.gov/const/mdbquery

The Federal Judiciary Homepage
http://www.uscourts.gov

University of Oklahoma College of Law chronology of U.S. Historical Documents
http://www.law.ou.edu/hist

National Archives and Records Administration
http://www.nara.gov

For Further Reading

Anderson, Jack. *Inside the NRA: Armed and Dangerous.* Beverly Hills, CA: Dove Books, 1996.

Bode, Janet, and Stan Mack. *Hard Time: A Real-Life Look at Juvenile Crime and Violence.* New York: Bantam Books, 1998.

Carter, Gregg Lee. *The Gun Control Movement.* New York: Twayne Publishers, 1997.

Hanson, Freya Ottem. *The Second Amendment: The Right to Own Guns.* Springfield, NJ: Enslow Publishers, 1998.

Jacobs, Nancy R., Normal Jones, and Mark A. Siegel. (eds.). *Gun Control: An American Issue.* Wylie, TX: Information Plus, 1997.

Kreiner, Anna. *Everything You Need to Know About School Violence.* New York: Rosen Publishing Group, 2000.

Kruschke, Earl R. *Gun Control: A Reference Handbook.* Santa Barbara, CA: ABC-Clio, 1995.

Lawrence, Richard. *School Crime and Juvenile Justice.*
New York: Oxford University Press, 1997.

Malcolm, Joyce Lee. *To Keep and Bear Arms: The Origins of an Anglo-American Right.* Cambridge, MA: Harvard University Press, 1996.

Miller, Maryann. *Coping with Weapons and Violence at School and on Your Streets.* New York: Rosen Publishing Group, 1999.

Roleff, Tamara L. (ed.). *Gun Control: Opposing Viewpoints.* Greenhaven Press: San Diego, 1997.

Schleifer, Jay, and Ruth C. Rosen (ed.). *Everything You Need to Know About Weapons in School and at Home.* New York: Rosen Publishing Group, 1999.

Sheley, Joseph F., and James D. Wright. *In the Line of Fire: Youths, Guns, and Violence in Urban America.* New York: Aldine de Gruyter, 1995.

Index

Credits

Series Design

Danielle Goldblatt

Layout

Les Kanturek